STRAYING FROM THE STRAIGHT PATH

Studies in Social Analysis
General Editor: Martin Holbraad
University College London

Focusing on analysis as a meeting ground of the empirical and the conceptual, this series provides a platform for exploring anthropological approaches to social analysis while seeking to open new avenues of communication between anthropology and the humanities, as well as other social sciences.

STRAYING FROM THE STRAIGHT PATH
How Senses of Failure Invigorate Lived Religion

Edited by

Daan Beekers and David Kloos

berghahn
NEW YORK · OXFORD
www.berghahnbooks.com

First published in 2018 by
Berghahn Books
www.berghahnbooks.com

© 2018, 2020 Daan Beekers and David Kloos
First paperback edition published in 2020

Library of Congress Cataloging-in-Publication Data

Names: Beekers, Daan, editor | Kloos, David, editor.
Title: Straying from the straight path : how senses of failure invigorate
  lived religion / edited by Daan Beekers and David Kloos.
Description: 1st [edition]. | New York : Berghahn Books, 2017. | Series:
  Studies in social analysis ; Volume 3 | Includes bibliographical
  references and index.
Identifiers: LCCN 2017037774 (print) | LCCN 2017039750 (ebook) | ISBN
  9781785337147 (ebook) | ISBN 9781785337130 (hardback : alk. paper)
Subjects: LCSH: Failure (Psychology)--Religious aspects. | Christianity and
  other religions--Islam. | Islam--Relations--Christianity.
Classification: LCC BL629.5.F33 (ebook) | LCC BL629.5.F33 S77 2017 (print) |
  DDC 202/.2--dc23
  LC record available at https://lccn.loc.gov/2017037774

British Library Cataloguing in Publication Data

A catalogue record for this book is available from the British Library

ISBN 978-1-78533-713-0 (hardback)
ISBN 978-1-78920-760-6 (paperback)
ISBN 978-1-78533-714-7 (ebook)

CONTENTS

Chapter 6
Moral Failure, Everyday Religion, and Islamic Authorization

PREFACE

The origin of this volume lies in a critical stance toward current anthropological debates about the religious lives of both Muslims and Christians. In the past decade, studies of pious pursuits have become pitted against studies that emphasize the incoherence of everyday religious lives. This book seeks to move beyond this dichotomy. It focuses on experiences of moral failure in order to explore how religious pursuits are shaped in interaction with, rather than apart from, the contradictions and uncertainties of everyday life.

We are grateful to Bruce Kapferer and Knut Mikjel Rio, former editors of *Social Analysis*, and their assistant Nora Haukali, who showed an initial interest in this work, and to the current editor, Martin Holbraad, who took over as the project was underway. We are also grateful to Vivian Berghahn for her close involvement during the final stages of the project. In addition, we acknowledge the assistance of all those at Berghahn Books who helped in bringing this volume to publication, including Caroline Kuhtz, Ben Parker and Kristyn Sanito. We also thank Sarah Sibley for her careful copy-editing of the manuscript. Finally, we thank the anonymous reviewer, whose comments helped us to improve the volume significantly.

INTRODUCTION
The Productive Potential of Moral Failure in Lived Islam and Christianity

David Kloos and Daan Beekers

This volume investigates the dialectical relationship between pursuits of religious coherence and experiences of moral fragmentation by focusing on self-perceived senses of failure. Our premise is that senses of failure offer an important and productive entry point for the study of lived religion in today's world, where religious commitments are often volatile, believers are regularly confronted by alternative lifestyles, worldviews or desires, and religious subjects tend to be self-reflexive. While the experience of failure in religious life has always been a central theme in theology and religious thought, it has long received little attention in the study of lived religion by anthropologists and others. In recent years, however, there has been a growing interest in various modes and moments of (self-perceived) failure, including feelings of incoherence and imperfection in religious life (Lechkar 2012; De Koning 2013; Jouili 2015; Strhan 2015), uncertainty about one's religious identity and the risk of falling back on pre-conversion relationships or habits (Marshall 2009; Pype 2011), doubt about religious truth claims (Luhrmann 2012; Liberatore 2013), ambivalent moral commitments (Schielke 2015), suspension or lack of religious meaning (Engelke and Tomlinson 2006), and unsuccessful careers of aspiring religious leaders (Lauterbach 2008).

We focus on Islam and Christianity, not only because these are the main religious traditions in terms of adherents, but also because the anthropology of

Islam and the anthropology of Christianity have in recent years seen reconfigurations that speak to the question of moral failure in crucial ways. A dichotomy has emerged in this literature between two broad positions (in sketching these positions, we do of course acknowledge the heterogeneity of approaches in each one of these): on the one hand, a strong focus has been developed on the cultivation of religious virtues and dispositions, as taking place in the context of religious activist movements, moments of (mass) conversion, and other instances in which religious truth claims take center stage (see, e.g., Harding 2000; Robbins 2004; Mahmood 2005; Hirschkind 2006). On the other hand, a growing body of literature has taken a critical stance toward this emphasis on the pursuit of ethical perfection in anthropological work. By pointing out the tensions, struggles, paradoxes, contradictions and ambivalences central to processes and instances of religious revival, conversion or the cultivation of piety, these studies challenge the suggestion, explicitly or implicitly advanced within the other perspective, that Muslims and Christians lead coherent, consistent or stable religious lives (see, e.g., Marsden 2005; Scott 2005; Engelke and Tomlinson 2006; Soares and Osella 2009; Schielke 2015). Indeed, the relatively recent interest in failure in religious life on the part of anthropologists can at least in part be seen as a response to the turn to personal piety and ethical formation in the anthropologies of Islam and Christianity.

We embrace the heightened attention for the contingency of everyday religious practices and experiences. Yet, we are critical of the tendency we observe in this scholarship to maintain a separation between religious practices and aspirations on the one hand and alternative moral frameworks or the sobering realities of everyday life on the other. Such an approach risks analytically placing experiences of imperfection and incoherence outside of the domain of religious experience "proper," rather than examining the dynamic and productive interactions between the two. By contrast, we aim to explore how, and to what extent, self-perceived failure is part and parcel of processes of ethical formation in lived Christianity and Islam. We suggest that senses of failure—defined as experiences that religious adherents themselves understand in terms of shortcoming, inadequacy, or imperfection, and that may include feelings of struggle, the perception of sins, negligence of religious obligations, and lack of religious confidence, faith, or belief—constitute a useful avenue for further developing the anthropology of Islam and Christianity in a broader framework of the anthropology of religion. The central question of this book, then, is how senses of failure feed back into Islamic and Christian ethical formation, by which we mean attempts at becoming "good" or "better" Muslims or Christians.

In contrast to the hitherto largely separated fields of the anthropology of Islam and Christianity, this volume approaches the problem of failure comparatively. We seek to move beyond the bifurcated study of religion (Soares 2006; Beekers 2014; Janson and Meyer 2016), by taking a particular concern—in our case everyday experiences of failure in religious life—as a productive entry point for an analysis of lived religion across religious boundaries. The next two sections serve to position this volume in current debates about the study of religious practice and ethical self-formation within the anthropologies of Islam and Christianity. By placing these debates side by side, we trace similar—though not identical—developments in each of these research fields. The subsequent section elaborates our proposition that self-perceived senses of failure are often constitutive of the ways in which many Muslims and Christians shape their faith. We close by introducing the individual contributions, each of which discusses different—but complementary and mutually enriching—dimensions of the role of failure in ethical formation.

We should note that there is neither space nor need to present comprehensive overviews of the anthropologies of Islam and Christianity here (see Kreinath [2012] for a recent overview on the anthropology of Islam, and Robbins [2014] for one on the anthropology of Christianity). Our intention is rather to point out similar debates in both fields about the primacy and effectiveness of religious modes of self-fashioning and world-making. We should also point out that, for the purposes of this volume, we have found it unnecessary to make an analytical distinction between the concepts of ethics and morality, as is often (though in different ways) done in philosophy and sometimes in anthropology (e.g., Zigon 2008). We agree with Michael Lambek (2010: 9) that, due to the disparate distinctions made between ethics and morality, opting for one of these—let alone introducing our own—risks creating more, rather than less, confusion.

The Question of Piety in the Anthropology of Islam

The anthropology of Islam has been concerned, from its early beginnings, with the relationship between particular (or locally specific) expressions of Islam and the complex of texts, scholarly disciplines and rituals that is generally, and across cultural and geographic boundaries, referred to as "Islam" or "Islamic." On the question of how to approach this relationship, conceptually and methodologically, positions have varied (see, e.g., Geertz 1968; El-Zein 1977, Eickelman 1982; Asad 1986). Particularly relevant for our purposes is Talal Asad's (1986) influential argument that Islam constitutes a "discursive tradition," and that religious disciplinary practices (or what he called, following Marcel Mauss, "body techniques") play a central role in the creation of religious subjects, and must be treated, analytically, as a mode of agency (Asad 1993).

Asad's framework has been put to use most effectively in the study of the "Islamic revival," a category of different socioreligious movements emerging since the 1970s, and engaging, one way or another, with the goal of strengthening and propagating the faith, often (but not always) in combination with a literalist approach to Islamic norms and a commitment to increase or "restore" the role of Islam in the public sphere. In her influential study of the revivalist women's "mosque movement" in Cairo, Egypt, Saba Mahmood (2005) argued that through their religious practices and disciplining of their bodies these women exercise a particular kind of agency, even when they choose to adopt the "non-liberal" and patriarchal notions of Muslim (feminine) personhood prevalent in the Islamic scriptural tradition (such as chastity, shyness, modesty, endurance, and perseverance). Charles Hirschkind (2006), in his study of the use of recorded cassette sermons in Cairo, also made use of an Asadian framework, as he argued that the act of listening to sermons constitutes a virtuous practice, a mode of disciplining ethical selves "predicated on the developability of the body as an auditory instrument" (Hirschkind 2006: 79). Thus, both Mahmood and Hirschkind have been concerned with excavating the forms of agency implied in practices central to pious Muslims' attempts at reaching a state of ethical perfection, and with investigating the ways in which this agency is rooted in individual and communal engagements with the Islamic (textual) discourses disseminated by religious authorities.

We single out these studies because they have inspired an important trend in the anthropology of Islam, which is characterized by a turn to personal piety and a focus on practices of self-cultivation. Of chief concern is the centrality in the Islamic revival of the concept of da'wa (Islamic propagation, lit. to "call" or "summon"). Da'wa-based discourses are grounded in the proposition that Islam offers a complete way of life and that all Muslims have a duty to actively and consciously subscribe to and disseminate this perspective. Earlier, the popularity of da'wa-infused language was primarily a topic of political scientists seeking to explain the rise of political Islam (see, e.g., Roy 1996; Kepel 2002). The innovation of Mahmood and Hirschkind (and those inspired by them) was, for a large part, the fact that anthropologists began to take seriously da'wa-based, Islamist (and other distinctly normative) discourses as important sources of self-formation. This shift toward the study of pious agency includes collections on the "pursuit of certainty" (James 2003) and on Muslim piety (Turner 2008; Amir-Moazami, Jacobsen, and Malik 2011), ethnographies of Muslim women in urban public spheres in Beirut (Deeb 2006) and Kuala Lumpur (Frisk 2009), studies of (especially young female) Muslims in Europe (Jouili and Amir-Moazami 2006; Fadil 2008; Jacobsen 2011; Jouili 2015), as well as work on Islamic education in Egypt (Starrett 1998) and on Islamist movements in urban Pakistan (Iqtidar 2011).

However, this focus on pious discipline and activist attitudes has also become the subject of mounting critique. Three, closely related, issues stand out. Firstly, it has been argued that the focus on the pursuit of ethical perfection presents the views and practices of a specific group—typically a minority segment of the urban middle class—as representative of observant Muslims. In the words of Magnus Marsden (2005: 9n), this distortion is accompanied by the problematic assumption that "'revivalist' Islam is the most powerful dimension of Muslim thought and identity in the contemporary Muslim world." And as Samuli Schielke (2010: 2) put it, the emphasis has been "on the very pious in moments when they are being very pious." Secondly, the narrowing down of the lives of Muslims to the cultivation of pious selves—including the implicit or explicit suggestion that Islam's foundational texts are the only or primary source of moral values for Muslims—has been said to constitute a case of ethnographic poverty. As one of Mahmood's reviewers put it, "her focus on the micro-practices inside the mosque seems to prevent her from looking at the micro-practices outside the mosque, since she does not follow the women she studies through all their various encounters with education and media," or "[relate] religious practices to the social fabric of Cairo" (Van der Veer 2008: 812; cf. Schielke 2010; Bangstad 2011). The studies on Muslim piety, in other words, have been criticized for their failure to address the ways in which religious practices and dispositions are shaped and compromised by the social, political and economic contexts in which these are embedded.

Thirdly, it has been argued that the religious lives of most Muslims are not governed by an internally coherent ethics or by a certainty about the place of religion in both public and private spheres. This is not so much a plea to contrast "revivalist" Muslims with people "unaffected" by religious transformation as it is an argument against the interpretation of the contemporary Islamic revival as a pervasive, uniform or constant force. Moving away from a focus on normative Islam and pursuits of ethical perfection, anthropologists working in different Muslim societies have highlighted the prevalence of moral ambivalence (Peletz 1997; Fischer 2008), the ways in which individual believers deal with and oscillate between conflicting "moral registers" (Schielke 2015: 53ff.), the complex process of making "ethical decisions" and the role of Islam therein (Marsden 2005: 260–62), and the tensions involved in the construction of "unstable" (Marsden and Retsikas 2013b: 8) or "multidimensional" (Simon 2014) selves.

One of the implications of this shift away from a focus on discipline is a general reframing of the anthropology of Islam in terms of broader ethnographic inquiries into Muslims' reflexive, creative and affective engagements with the world in which they live (Marsden 2005; Soares and Osella 2009; Schielke and Debevec 2012; Dessing et al. 2013). The studies cited above observe that many (or most) Muslims do not, or at least not primarily or continually, engage in the cultivation of a "pious self." They do not "walk around in a religious bubble," as Nancy Ammerman (2014: 194) stated in reference to religious adherents generally, but are rather driven by a range of concerns, desires, and interests—the "changing and often contradictory quandaries of everyday life," as Marsden and Retsikas (2013b: 8) put it—of which the aspiration to engage in pious practice is an aspect, not a sole determinant. The important point is that religiosity cannot be detached from this broader context of multifaceted and often unpredictable everyday lives. Yet, it is precisely on this point that we signal a tendency within this body of work to maintain an, in our view, unhelpful separation between the pursuit of religious coherence on the one hand and the fragmentation of everyday life on the other.

There is a resemblance between our discussion of this literature and Nadia Fadil and Mayanthi Fernando's (2015) recent polemical critique, directed primarily at the work of Schielke. The turn to "everyday Islam," they argue, has created a problematic opposition between "piety" and "the everyday." The proponents of this turn "conceptualize normative doctrine and everyday practice as unconnected and, indeed, as opposed. Yet, the fact that a commitment

to a particular norm is often imperfectly achieved does not refute the importance attached to that norm" (ibid.: 70). Although our critique resonates with
theirs, we approach the debate differently. Unlike Fadil and Fernando, we
believe that the critical response to "the piety turn" (2015: 81) does offer an
important corrective by acknowledging the complexity and multiplicity of
everyday lives. Fadil and Fernando mention that their aim is not to invalidate
this critical body of work. Yet they do in fact question its very postulates and
maintain that everyday practices had already been given ample attention in the
study of Islamic piety (ibid.: 65)—an observation we do not share. We also dis-
agree with their claim that the focus on the everyday privileges or presupposes
resistance to norms (at least, we do not see this in Schielke's work, on which
much of their criticism rests).

In her response to Fadil and Fernando's piece, Lara Deeb (2015) suggests a
helpful way to move this debate forward. She proposes to think "piety and the
everyday together" by examining "both the ways the everyday is shaped by
religious discipline and normativity *and* the ways that religious discipline and
normativity are themselves produced through and change via everyday social
life" (ibid.: 96; emphasis in the original; cf. Elliot 2016). We follow a similar
line of inquiry by tracing the ways in which experiences of fragmentation in
everyday life can be found to affect and even invigorate the pursuit of religious
ideals. Before moving on to elaborate on this, however, we will show that
this debate is not only relevant to the anthropology of Islam. The maturation
within the past decade or so of an "anthropology of Christianity" has entailed
similarly opposed positions.

The Question of Coherence in the Anthropology of Christianity

The "anthropology of Christianity" has only recently been developed as a
field in and of itself—that is, a field characterized by a degree of theoretical
and conceptual coherence, a global comparative perspective, and a sense of
academic community (see especially Robbins 2003 and 2014). Self-consciously
modelled on the longer existing "anthropology of Islam" (Robbins 2003, 2007;
Garriott and O'Neill 2008), the anthropology of Christianity is driven by the
view that anthropologists have, for various reasons, neglected the relevance
of Christianity as a culturally constitutive force in the lives of the people
they studied. The proponents of this field, many of whom are researchers of
non-Western societies that have seen (mass) conversions to Christianity, argue
that full attention should be given to the ways in which Christian theological
models, textual traditions and embodied practices shape local communities
and individual subjectivities (Cannell 2006b; Engelke and Tomlinson 2006;
Robbins 2007; Jenkins 2012).

The work of Webb Keane (1997, 2007) constitutes an important early contribution to this discussion. In his analysis of conversion in Sumba, Indonesia,
he shows that the adoption of Calvinist ideas challenged and transformed
indigenous *(marapu)* concepts of agency. Indicating the Protestant insistence

on replacing objects by language as the main locus or signifier of divine agency, Keane argues that Protestant conversion served to "draw a clear line between humans and nonhumans, between the world of agency and that of natural determinism" (2007: 7). A similar position has been developed by Joel Robbins (2004) in his work on the Urapmin, a highland community in Papua New Guinea. Like Keane, he is interested in exploring the relationship between "inner" beliefs and changing moral and social orders. Religious experience, Robbins argues, must be regarded as a driver of cultural change. While Robbins does not deny the influence of political and economic factors, he makes a powerful argument for taking seriously the emotional concern of the second coming (central to the Urapmin's attachment to a form of millenarian Christianity) as a force that shapes the ways in which people organize their society and lead their lives.

Thus, an important trend within this budding field has been—in line with Keane, Robbins, and other influential contributors (e.g., Harding 2000)—the analytical move to give full attention to Christian culture and theology "in their own right" (Chua 2012: 12). The proponents of this perspective claim that earlier work tended to perceive Christianity as a second-order phenomenon: a tool of economic or political gain, or a superficial, foreign construct superimposed on a more "authentic" indigenous culture (Cannell 2006a; Robbins 2007; Jenkins 2012). The "non-reductive" approach to Christianity that is advocated instead has been strongly formulated by Ruth Marshall (2009) in her work on "Born Again" Pentecostals in Nigeria (itself not presented as a contribution to the anthropology of Christianity). "Religious change," she writes, "is not merely the sign or the effect of change in other domains of human practice, but constitutes rather, in and of itself, a mode of historical and political transformation" (2009: 34). Accordingly, Marshall draws attention to the ways in which Pentecostalism shapes particular moral and political subjects. A central trope in this field, then, is discontinuity, denoting the transformative consequences of Christian belief, practice and tradition within social communities and people's individual lives, particularly through narratives of conversion, rebirth, and historical rupture (Robbins 2007; Marshall 2009; Engelke and Robbins 2010).

Yet, this scholarly quest for an analysis of Christianity as a force of cultural change has been shot through with critical voices. Even some of the protagonists of this new field have expressed doubts as to whether Christianity can be studied as a coherent religious tradition (Cannell 2006b; Engelke and Tomlinson 2006). A first issue raised in these critical contributions is the great diversity of manifestations of Christianity across different sociohistorical contexts. Thus, Fenella Cannell points out that her edited volume *The Anthropology of Christianity* provides "accounts of particular, local Christianities as they are lived" (2006a: 5), while Michael Scott calls for distinguishing between local variations of Christianity by examining "ethno-theologies" by which (convert) Christians "evaluate indigenous ideas and practices in relation to those of Christianity and situate ancestral identities and histories within biblical history" (2005: 102).

A second key point of critique of the notion of Christianity as a force of cultural change is that such transformative power of religion is limited because of (long-standing) economic and political conditions. Debra McDougall (2009) makes this argument in her critical discussion of Robbins' description of the onset of individualism among the Urapmin as a result of their conversion to Christianity. She draws attention to Robbins' insight of a disjuncture between the new ideology of the Urapmin and the unchanged material and social conditions of their lives, arguing that "[r]egardless of how much Urapmin would like to overthrow the trappings of their old way of life and embrace what they understand to be the unrelenting individualism of Christianity, this desire alone will not make them individuals until their mode of subsistence changes" (ibid.: 15). Ruth Marshall makes a similar point when she states that the transformative project of Pentecostalism in Nigeria can never be fully achieved, because it cannot overcome long-standing modes of kinship, political organization and economic relations. Instead, the "prescriptive regime" of Pentecostalism remains largely "strategic and programmatic" (2009: 10–11), retaining its force as a promise and potentiality. Note, here, that quite similar arguments have been made with regard to the future-oriented (and ultimately rather impracticable) attempts of revivalist Muslims to create a "perfect" Islamic society (see, e.g., Feener 2013).

In their volume on "the limits of meaning" in the lives and rituals of Christians, Engelke and Tomlinson (2006) have pointed out the instabilities within Christian ideology itself. They argue that if "ultimate religious meaning" constitutes a key theme in lived Christianity (cf. Robbins 2003), then this "emphasis on meaning entails the potential of its absence, negation, or irrelevance" (Tomlinson and Engelke 2006: 23). Instances of failure, such as a ritual going wrong because the words or acts are not remembered, allow scholars to "approach meaning not as a function or as a product to be uncovered, but as a process and potential fraught with uncertainty and contestation" (ibid.: 2).

A third concern with regard to the focus on Christianity "per se" (Hann 2007) parallels the criticisms of the turn to piety in the anthropology of Islam; it is that the personal lives as well as the social worlds of Christian believers entail much more than religious concerns alone. Simon Coleman (2013: 255), among others, has pointed out that studies in the anthropology of Christianity have focused on committed, often evangelical, Christians and their religious practices, while activities that take up a great part of most Christians' lives—such as work and leisure—are often given (much) less attention. Katrien Pype puts it succinctly in her work on born-again Christians in Kinshasa: "Social life in Kinshasa makes it impossible to be a 'perfect' Christian all the time" (2011: 301; cf. Strhan 2015). Adding a cultural historical dimension to this, Liana Chua (2012) shows that the Bidayuh in Malaysia have converted to Christianity in large numbers but still seek to maintain continuity with their "old rituals" (adat gawai). In the next section, we show how an analysis of widespread experiences of moral failure may open up new critical perspectives within the anthropology of Christianity and Islam.

Moral Failure and Ethical Formation

While the anthropology of Islam and the anthropology of Christianity have for a large part developed separately from one another (despite the latter having taken the former as its model), we signal a common debate at the heart of both. On the one hand, scholars have posited that Islam and Christianity provide—what we will here call—distinct ethical "scripts" that, once adopted and acted upon, strongly affect the ways in which people live their lives. They argue that these scripts, emanating from textual interpretation, theological debates, and the interaction between ordinary believers and religious authorities, should be taken seriously in ethnographic studies of religious modes of self-fashioning and world-making. This position has been significantly strengthened by the organization of the anthropology of Islam and Christianity as distinct fields of study. On the other hand, researchers critical of the position that analytical primacy should be given to religious tradition have warned against placing disproportionate emphasis on such religious modes of self-fashioning and world-making. They point out that Muslims and Christians are generally affected as much by "nonreligious" ethical scripts and dispositions as by religious ethics. Religious aspirations, they argue, often remain unfulfilled because of the contingencies of everyday life or because ordinary believers frequently prioritize other concerns.

In parts of the literature, especially within the anthropology of Islam (cf. Fadil and Fernando 2015), these two perspectives have tended to develop into opposite and even mutually exclusive positions. Even analyses that give explicit attention to both perspectives tend to maintain a separation between the fields of "religion proper" and "lived reality," or between religious moral frameworks and nonreligious ones. Thus, Samuli Schielke (2015: 53ff.) emphasizes the separate "moral registers" that rural Egyptians draw on as they shift between different social contexts and move from one life stage to the next. Benjamin Soares and Filippo Osella (2009: S12), on their part, advanced the concept of "Islam mondain" to analyze how Muslim practices of self-fashioning draw simultaneously on Islam and on a desire to be, or to become, "modern" (implying a range of essentially non- or not necessarily religious concerns related to "politics, morality, family, consumption, employment, media, entertainment, and so forth"). We agree with the observation that religious believers often distinguish between religious and nonreligious domains, drawing from both as sources of moral subjectivity. Yet, we feel that analyses of ethical formation in both the anthropologies of Islam and Christianity have not given sufficient attention to the dynamic and productive *interactions* between religious and nonreligious concerns, moral frameworks, and practices.

The goal of this book is to move beyond this dichotomy by taking the interplay between religious aspirations and the contingencies of everyday life as a point of departure for our ethnographic analyses. Our approach may be viewed in relation to a number of recent attempts to explore the effects of, and creativity inherent in, expressions of moral uncertainty, doubt, and imperfection. A notable example is Oskar Verkaaik's (2014) study of the architecture of synagogues in Germany and the Netherlands, in which he draws attention to the ways in which senses of "rupture," or "everyday degradation," are integrated in the design of these buildings. He makes a case for taking seriously the "religious art of imperfection"—that is, for seeing "modern religiosity ... as an ongoing engagement with a fragmented and unsettled reality, both historically and existentially" and for "develop[ing] a view on how modern religious subjects deal with and incorporate imperfection" (ibid.: 488). Yet, in addition to Verkaaik's inquiry into the ways in which religious adherents address and cope with failure, we are concerned with the question of how self-perceived senses of failure feed back into pursuits of religious coherence and truth, or in other words, how senses of failure constitute productive grounds for believers to reflect and work on their moral selves. To put it differently, we are interested in what Matt Tomlinson and Matthew Engelke term "the productive potentialities of failure, misunderstanding, ignorance, chaos, and uncertainty" (2006: 26n).

Our approach builds on the recent volumes by Elizabeth Cooper and David Pratten on the "productive potential of uncertainty" (2015: 1) and by Mathijs Pelkmans (2013a) on the ethnography of doubt. Uncertainty, according to Cooper and Pratten (2015: 2), may be approached as a "social resource" and a "source for imagining the future"—and, as such, as a basis for action (cf. Horst and Grabska 2015). Doubt, according to Pelkmans, energizes human thought and action. He argues that "doubt and belief should not be seen as opposites, but rather as co-constitutive parts" (Pelkmans 2013b: 4). Thus, "convictions are not simply present, but are rather produced in dialogue with challenges (challenges which may take the form of doubt)" (ibid.: 26). In her contribution to Pelkmans' volume, Giulia Liberatore (2013) shows that her interlocutors—young Somali Muslim women in London who have only recently started to practice Islam—occasionally suffer from doubts about the after-worldly rewards for their efforts and sacrifices in this world. These anxieties, Liberatore argues, do not only threaten their faith but also invigorate it. Within their communities of Muslim peers, these women learn to signify and manage their doubts as instances of "low *iman* [faith]," thereby encapsulating such doubts within their "system of faith" (ibid.: 245). Doubts, then, are acted upon and taken by these women as stimuli to strengthen their faith.

Another instructive account of religious doubt is provided by Tanya Luhrmann's (2012: 375) work on American evangelicals. She points out that these Christians are confronted by an inevitable presence of doubt and skepticism when it comes to "accepting God's real reality" (ibid.: 375). In their "secular-sited Christianity," faith is lived with "the acute awareness that one can choose not to believe—not only in this specific faith, but in the transcendent at all" (2012: 378). Luhrmann argues, however, that their doubt and skepticism trigger these evangelicals to cultivate a deliberately imaginative and playful experience of God. They effectively sidestep their doubts by construing a conception of a "hyper-real" God. Thus, for Luhrmann, the very inevitability of doubt and skepticism in these believers' lives fosters the creation of this particular kind of miraculous Christianity.

These accounts are innovative, because they show that religious doubts may not only impede but also have a revitalizing effect on religious belief and commitment. Building on earlier anthropological engagements with the constructive potential of uncertainty and doubt for religious beliefs (see, e.g., Goody 1996: 678; Engelke 2005: 783–84), Liberatore and Luhrmann investigate the intricate ways by which experiences of doubt serve to re-establish, retrace or invigorate religious convictions. The chapters collected in this book elaborate on these important insights by examining the ways in which not only doubt and uncertainty, but also (other kinds of) self-perceived shortcomings, practical struggles, sins or negligence may play a productive role within religious pursuits. While the recognition of, and response to, failure takes a central place in core doctrinal traditions in both Islam and Christianity, the varied ways in which senses of failure can be found to propel processes of ethical formation have—apart from the aforementioned studies—received too little attention in anthropological studies of everyday religious lives.

What counts as "moral failure" in our approach is what is experienced and designated as such by our interlocutors in the field. By this we do not mean to say, of course, that the definition of failure takes place in some kind of detached mode. Experiences of failure result from the individual and collective "grappling" with religious "texts, ideas and methods" (Bowen 2012: 3) under such contemporary social conditions as globalization, consumer capitalism, neoliberalism, and secularism (see, e.g., Soares and Osella 2009; Hefner 2010; Rudnyckyj 2010; Elisha 2011). Senses of failure, moreover, are embedded in the complex social, political and historically shaped interactions between individual believers and the normative forces—organized religion, states and religious bureaucracies, popular preachers, et cetera—that claim the authority to formulate and disseminate the "proper" content, the boundaries of religious traditions, its codes of conduct, and its routes to salvation (see, e.g., Eickelman and Piscatori 1996). As Thijl Sunier argues in his contribution to this volume, the focus on failure works in two ways. It allows investigating how religious adherents reflect and act upon religious norms and their own perceived shortcomings, but also how the engagement with religious norms, including reflections on perceived shortcomings, serve to "authenticate" and "authorize" particular interpretations and their proponents.

Before providing, in the final section, an outline of the individual contributions to this book, we will briefly comment on the connections between our project and the broader turn to the study of ethics in anthropology. While ethics has long been a concern of anthropologists, in recent years there has been a marked increase of attempts to deal with this dimension of human life in a more systematic way. Michael Lambek (2010: 9), for instance, has advanced the concept of "ordinary ethics," to denote "the ethical in the broader sense, referring to the field of action or practical judgment rather than to what is specifically right or good" (cf. Das 2007; Sykes 2008). Others have engaged with what Mahmood (2005) calls positive ethics—the (ritual or other) practices, or what Foucault termed "techniques of the self," through which particular virtues are cultivated (Asad 1993; Mahmood 2005; Hirschkind 2006; Faubion 2011). Others again have centralized the problem of how to distinguish or "locate" the realm of ethics within wider complexes of social and cultural structures and processes (Zigon 2008; Laidlaw 2014) and the question of how to approach specific moments of ethical formation in the lives of individual people (Zigon 2008; Mattingly 2014). This literature derives much of its urgency from the suggestion that the turn to ethics could inspire a reconfiguration of anthropology more broadly (see, e.g., Laidlaw 2014) and from the question of how anthropology might relate, productively and creatively, to other scholarly and scientific disciplines with strong traditions in the study of morality (Lambek 2010; Keane 2015).

The contributions to this volume speak to this literature in different ways, and it is not our intention to present another position in the debate over what an "anthropology of ethics" should entail. Yet, we emphasize that in their approaches to senses of failure among Muslims and Christians, the contributors rest neither with moral deliberation nor with techniques of the self as a dominant framework of analysis. Our interest in moral failure resonates with recent analyses of moral "perils" or "tragedies" (Mattingly 2014), suffering (Throop 2010), and especially Jarett Zigon's (2008: 165) conceptualization of "moral breakdown"; that is, instances in which people become—sometimes suddenly or unexpectedly, but nonetheless consciously and astutely—"reflective and reflexive about their moral being in the world" (ibid.). However, in contrast to Zigon's approach, which focuses on specific moments of failure that prompt people to act on their moral selves, most of the chapters collected here engage with senses of failure as a more recurrent feature of Muslims' and Christians' everyday religiosities. Our specific contribution is that we investigate the dialectical relationship between Muslims' and Christians' experiences of moral instability, fragmentation or ambivalence on the one hand and their attempts to achieve a level of moral coherence grounded in religion on the other.

The Contributions

The contributions to this book show that failure plays a central role in processes of ethical formation within both Islam and Christianity, and that it does so in many different ways. The first two chapters explore religious practices and narratives in which failure is purposively placed at the very heart of faith, rather than its margins. Joel Robbins and Leanne Williams Green explore a particularly prominent religious discourse on moral failure: the Christian conception of human fallenness grounded in the idea of original sin. Examining the ways in which experiences of sinfulness constitute a motivating force for engaging in religious practice, they begin by distinguishing between two different patterns of accounting for moral failure and sinfulness in Pentecostal and charismatic Christianity: an "internal" pattern that attributes individuals' susceptibility to sinning to their personal moral shortcomings, and an "external" pattern that takes sinfulness to be the result of demonic influence and temptation. These patterns are not mutually exclusive and may also appear in hybrid forms. Robbins and Williams Green subsequently argue that the particular conceptualization of sinfulness in Christian communities importantly affects Christian ritual life: the "internal" pattern motivates believers to invest in practices of moral self-improvement, while the "external" pattern tends to motivate practices of deliverance and protection against demonic powers. In both cases, as the authors put it with regard to Urapmin Christianity, the recognition of human failure can be seen as "the engine of their Christian ritual life."

Martijn de Koning examines what Robbins and Williams Green might describe as an "internal" pattern of understanding human failure among Salafi Muslims in the Netherlands. While his interlocutors assert that Salafism is the only correct and true version of Islam, they simultaneously present themselves as "weak servants." Examining this paradox, De Koning turns the common view of moral inadequacy as an impediment to piety upside down. He shows that senses of failure form an innate part of Salafi practices and discourses of ethical cultivation, stimulating Salafis to improve their personal piety. Thus, among Dutch Salafi Muslims the state of weakness "gains a virtuous moral value." By presenting themselves as weak and failing in interaction with others, moreover, they are able to fashion themselves as "sincere" Muslims, who recognize their shortcomings and strive to become better Muslims.

In the third chapter, Linda van de Kamp discusses Christians in Mozambique who attend Brazilian Pentecostal churches and adhere to the "Prosperity Gospel" propagated within these churches. Several of her interlocutors, however, fail to realize the promises of prosperity in their lives: rather than an increase of economic success and happiness, their (financial) sacrifices to the church bring about downward economic mobility and an unhappy family life. Van de Kamp shows how these experiences are framed by a strong discourse of personal responsibility that focuses on her interlocutors' own perceived lack of religious determination and sincerity. She shows that the adverse effects of Pentecostal adherence do not stimulate them to turn away from faith, but rather to develop a "rational" or "intelligent" faith. By emphasizing notions of personal responsibility, Van de Kamp draws attention to the important question of how (both worldly and religious) failure is accounted for. This issue of responsibility, which Robbins and Williams Green describe as failure's "unexpected sibling," emerges in several chapters collected in this volume. Van de Kamp argues that her interlocutors' focus on personal responsibility indicates that their Pentecostal Christianity dovetails with the increasingly neoliberal economy of Mozambique.

Daan Beekers also looks at the ways in which religious pursuits interact with a neoliberal, capitalist economy. He shows that young Sunni Muslims and Protestant Christians in the Netherlands struggle with feelings of inadequacy and failure because they often do not manage to make as much time for prayer and other worship practices as they want to. Beekers argues that these struggles should be understood in the context of the quickened pace of life in today's fast capitalist culture in the Netherlands. In his analysis, however, there is more to the dynamics between religion and capitalism than mere antagonism. He demonstrates that fast capitalist culture also endows his interlocutors' worship practices with a renewed value, as these practices are felt to bring about tranquility and thereby a release from the very acceleration of everyday life. By explicitly analyzing Muslims and Christians within one framework, Beekers' contribution shows most directly that an inquiry into everyday struggles under particular social conditions allows for a productive analysis across different religions.

The theme of failure in worship is also the central concern in David Kloos' chapter on prayer in rural Aceh, Indonesia. He seeks to explain why, in a part of Indonesia where public discourses of Islamic morality are particularly strong, the negligence in prayer among some of his interlocutors raised so little disapproval within the village community. Closely examining the case of a young man with an outstanding reputation as someone who "didn't pray," Kloos argues that his negligence in prayer did not signal a lack of faith, but rather an "uncultivated faith," contingent on a broadly shared ethical mode centered on expectations and hopes of future self-improvement. In this religious ethics, it is the intention to improve oneself that counts above all—a concern that these Acehnese villagers share with the more reformist Muslims in De Koning's contribution. Kloos further shows that the emphasis on personal responsibility not only makes religious endeavors more demanding, but also allows for flexibility. Here, then, moral flexibility and ambivalence are shown to result not only from the quandaries of everyday life but also from a particular kind of religious ethics.

Thijl Sunier further elaborates on the question of maneuvering space in ethical practice. Compared to the other contributions, his analysis more explicitly centralizes a collective level and what he terms the "total ethical scheme," of which senses of failure may or may not be part. Sunier draws attention to the question when—and under influence of what kind of developments, situations or events—something comes to be defined as moral failure. Focusing on everyday religious experiences of Muslims in Western Europe, he argues that while the frictions and dilemmas they experience as a result of changing social conditions often bring about senses of failure, they may also trigger a reflexive reconsideration of the normative frames that undergird the very evaluation of failure and success. Thus, he argues that the study of moral failure also necessarily involves an inquiry into religious authority. While moral dilemmas often work to reproduce or affirm religious authority, in some cases they lead to its reconfiguration.

The collection closes with an epilogue in which Mattijs van de Port responds to the ideas put forward in the contributions to this book. Extending the volume's central premise that moral failure is part and parcel of religious modes of self-fashioning, he argues that experiences of failure can be understood to be inherent to all human world-making, be it religious or otherwise. Van de Port suggests two trajectories for further research—one based on Lacanian thought, the other on affect theory—that could be undertaken to analyze failure as an "authentically" human experience. Taken together, the contributions to this volume show that experiences of contingency and pursuits of religious coherence cannot be seen as separate or isolated domains of action or consciousness. They actively influence and operate on each other, producing religious subjectivities in the process.

Acknowledgments

We thank Victor Kal, Birgit Meyer, Bruno Reinhardt, Annemarie Samuels, Pooyan Tamimi Arab, and an anonymous reviewer for their helpful comments on a draft of this chapter. We are also grateful for the useful questions and suggestions we received during a research colloquium at the Department of Philosophy and Religious Studies at Utrecht University.

David Kloos is a senior researcher at the Royal Netherlands Institute of Southeast Asian and Caribbean Studies (KITLV) in Leiden, The Netherlands. He is the author of *Becoming Better Muslims: Religious Authority and Ethical Improvement in Aceh, Indonesia* (Princeton University Press).

Daan Beekers is a social anthropologist currently affiliated with the Alwaleed Centre for the Study of Islam in the Contemporary World, University of Edinburgh. His first monograph, an ethnographic study of religious commitment among young Muslims and Christians in the Netherlands, is forthcoming with Bloomsbury.

References

Amir-Moazami, Schirin, Christine M. Jacobsen, and Maleiha Malik, eds. 2011. "Special Issue: Islam and Gender in Europe: Subjectivities, Politics and Piety." *Feminist Review* 98(1).

Ammerman, Nancy T. 2014. "Finding Religion in Everyday Life (2013 Paul Hanly Furfey Lecture)." *Sociology of Religion* 75(2): 189–207.

Asad, Talal. 1986. "The Idea of an Anthropology of Islam." *Occasional papers series*. Washington, D.C.: Georgetown University Center for Contemporary Arab Studies.

———. 1993. *Genealogies of Religion: Discipline and Reasons of Power in Christianity and Islam.* Baltimore, MD: Johns Hopkins University Press.

Bangstad, Sindre. 2011. "Saba Mahmood and Anthropological Feminism after Virtue." *Theory, Culture & Society* 28(3): 28–54.

Beekers, Daan. 2014. "Pedagogies of Piety: Comparing Young Observant Muslims and Christians in the Netherlands." *Culture and Religion* 15(1): 72–99.

Bowen, John R. 2012. *A New Anthropology of Islam.* Cambridge: Cambridge University Press.

Cannell, Fenella. 2006a. "Introduction: The Anthropology of Christianity." In *The Anthropology of Christianity,* ed. Fenella Cannel, 1–50. Durham, NC: Duke University Press.

Cannell, Fenella., ed. 2006b. *The Anthropology of Christianity.* Durham, NC: Duke University Press.

Chua, Liana. 2012. *The Christianity of Culture: Conversion, Ethnic Citizenship, and the Matter of Religion in Malaysian Borneo.* New York: Palgrave Macmillan.

Coleman, Simon. 2013. "Afterword: De-exceptionalising Islam." In *Articulating Islam: Anthropological Approaches to Muslim Worlds,* ed. Magnus Marsden and Konstantinos Retsikas, 247–258. Dordrecht: Springer Science & Business Media.

Cooper, Elizabeth, and David Pratten. 2015. "Ethnographies of Uncertainty in Africa: An Introduction." In *Ethnographies of Uncertainty in Africa,* ed. Elizabeth Cooper and David Pratten, 1–16. Basingstoke: Palgrave Macmillan.

Das, Veena. 2007. *Life and Words: Violence and the Descent into the Ordinary.* Berkeley, CA: University of California Press.

Deeb, Lara. 2006. *An Enchanted Modern: Gender and Public Piety in Shi'i Lebanon.* Princeton, NJ: Princeton University Press.

———. 2015. "Thinking Piety and the Everyday Together: A Response to Fadil and Fernando." *HAU: Journal of Ethnographic Theory* 5(2): 93–96.

De Koning, Martijn. 2013. "The Moral Maze: Dutch Salafis and the Construction of a Moral Community of the Faithful." *Contemporary Islam* 7(1): 71–83.

Dessing, Nathal M., Nadia Jeldtoft, Jørgen S. Nielsen, and Linda Woodhead, eds. 2013. *Everyday Lived Islam in Europe.* Farnham and Burlington, VT: Ashgate.

Eickelman, Dale F. 1982. "The Study of Islam in Local Contexts." *Contributions to Asian Studies* 17: 1–16.

Eickelman, Dale F., and James Piscatori. 1996. *Muslim Politics.* Princeton, NJ: Princeton University Press.

Elisha, Omri. 2011. *Moral Ambition: Mobilization and Social Outreach in Evangelical Megachurches.* Berkeley, CA: University of California Press.

Elliot, Alice. 2016. "The Makeup of Destiny: Predestination and the Labor of Hope in a Moroccan Emigrant Town." *American Ethnologist* 43(3): 488–499.

El-Zein, Abdul Hamid. 1977. "Beyond Ideology and Theology: The Search for the Anthropology of Islam." *Annual Review of Anthropology* 6(1): 227–254.

Engelke, Matthew E. 2005. "The Early Days of Johane Masowe: Self-Doubt, Uncertainty, and Religious Transformation." *Comparative Studies in Society and History* 47(4): 781–808.

Engelke, Matthew E., and Joel Robbins, eds. 2010. "Special Issue: Global Christianity, Global Critique." *South Atlantic Quarterly* 109(4).

Engelke, Matthew E., and Matt Tomlinson. 2006. *The Limits of Meaning: Case Studies in the Anthropology of Christianity.* New York and Oxford: Berghahn Books.

Fadil, Nadia. 2008. *Submitting to God, Submitting to the Self: Secular and Religious Trajectories of Second Generation Maghrebi in Belgium.* Ph.D. dissertation. KU Leuven.

Fadil, Nadia and Mayanthi Fernando. 2015. "Rediscovering the 'Everyday' Muslim: Notes on an Anthropological Divide." *HAU: Journal of Ethnographic Theory* 5(2): 59–88.

Faubion, James D. 2011. *An Anthropology of Ethics*. Cambridge: Cambridge University Press.

Feener, R. Michael. 2013. *Shari'a and Social Engineering: The Implementation of Islamic Law in Contemporary Aceh, Indonesia*. Oxford: Oxford University Press.

Fischer, Johan. 2008. *Proper Islamic Consumption: Shopping among the Malays in Modern Malaysia*. Copenhagen: NIAS press.

Frisk, Sylva. 2009. *Submitting to God: Women and Islam in Urban Malaysia*. Copenhagen: NIAS press.

Garriott, William, and Kevin Lewis O'Neill. 2008. "Who is a Christian? Toward a Dialogic Approach in the Anthropology of Christianity." *Anthropological Theory* 8(4): 381–398.

Geertz, Clifford. 1968. *Islam Observed*. New Haven, CT: Yale University Press.

Goody, Jack. 1996. "A Kernel of Doubt." *The Journal of the Royal Anthropological Institute* 2(4): 667–681.

Hann, Chris. 2007. "The Anthropology of Christianity Per Se." *European Journal of Sociology/Archives Européennes de Sociologie* 48(3): 383–410.

Harding, Susan Friend. 2000. *The Book of Jerry Falwell: Fundamentalist Language and Politics*. Princeton, NJ and Oxford: Princeton University Press.

Hefner, Robert W. 2010. "Religious Resurgence in Contemporary Asia: Southeast Asian Perspectives on Capitalism, the State, and the New Piety." *The Journal of Asian Studies* 69(4): 1031–1047.

Hirschkind, Charles. 2006. *The Ethical Soundscape: Cassette Sermons and Islamic Counterpublics*. New York: Columbia University Press.

Horst, Cindy, and Katarzyna Grabska. 2015. "Introduction: Flight and Exile – Uncertainty in the Context of Conflict-Induced Displacement." *Social Analysis* 59(1): 1–18.

Iqtidar, Humeira. 2011. *Secularizing Islamists? Jama'at-e-Islami and Jama'at-ud-Da'wa in Urban Pakistan*. Chicago: University of Chicago Press.

Jacobsen, Christine M. 2011. *Islamic Traditions and Muslim Youth in Norway*. Leiden and Boston, MA: Brill.

James, Wendy., ed. 2003. *The Pursuit of Certainty: Religious and Cultural Formulations*. London: Routledge.

Janson, Marloes, and Birgit Meyer, eds. 2016. "Special Issue: Studying Islam and Christianity in Africa: Moving Beyond a Bifurcated Field." *Africa* 86(4).

Jenkins, Timothy. 2012. "The Anthropology of Christianity: Situation and Critique." *Ethnos* 77(4): 459–476.

Jouili, Jeanette S. 2015. *Pious Practice and Secular Constraints: Women in the Islamic Revival in Europe*. Stanford, CA: Stanford University Press.

Jouili, Jeanette S., and Schirin Amir-Moazami. 2006. "Knowledge, Empowerment and Religious Authority among Pious Muslim Women in France and Germany." *The Muslim World* 96(4): 617–642.

Keane, Webb. 1997. "From Fetishism to Sincerity: On Agency, the Speaking Subject, and their Historicity in the Context of Religious Conversion." *Comparative Studies in Society and History* 39(4): 674–693.

———. 2007. *Christian Moderns: Freedom and Fetish in the Mission Encounter*. Berkeley, CA: University of California Press.

———. 2015. *Ethical Life: Its Natural and Social Histories*. Princeton, NJ: Princeton University Press.

Kepel, Gilles. 2002. *Jihad: The Trail of Political Islam*. Cambridge, MA: Belknap Press.

Kreinath, Jens., ed. 2012. *The Anthropology of Islam Reader*. Abingdon: Routledge.
Laidlaw, James. 2014. *The Subject of Virtue: An Anthropology of Ethics and Freedom*. Cambridge: Cambridge University Press.
Lambek, Michael J. 2010. "Introduction." In *Ordinary Ethics: Anthropology, Language, and Action*, ed. Michael Lambek, 1–36. New York: Fordham University Press.
Lauterbach, Karen. 2008. "The Craft of Pastorship in Ghana and Beyond." Ph.D. dissertation. Roskilde University.
Lechkar, Iman. 2012. "Striving and Stumbling in the Name of Allah: Neo-Sunnis and Neo-Shi'ites in a Belgian Context." Ph.D. dissertation. KU Leuven.
Liberatore, Giulia. 2013. "Doubt as a Double-Edged Sword: Unanswerable Questions and Practical Solutions among Newly Practising Somali Women in London." In *Ethnographies of Doubt: Faith and Uncertainty in Contemporary Societies*, ed. Mathijs Pelkmans, 225–250. New York: I.B. Tauris.
Luhrmann, Tanya M. 2012. "A Hyperreal God and Modern Belief." *Current Anthropology* 53(4): 371–395.
Mahmood, Saba. 2005. *Politics of Piety: The Islamic Revival and the Feminist Subject*. Princeton, NJ: Princeton University Press.
Marsden, Magnus. 2005. *Living Islam: Muslim Religious Experience in Pakistan's North-West Frontier*. Cambridge: Cambridge University Press.
Marsden, Magnus, and Konstantinos Retsikas, eds. 2013a. *Articulating Islam: Anthropological Approaches to Muslim Worlds*. Dordrecht: Springer Science & Business Media.
Marsden, Magnus, and Konstantinos Retsikas. 2013b. "Introduction." In *Articulating Islam: Anthropological Approaches to Muslim Worlds*, ed. Magnus Marsden and Konstantinos Retsikas, 1–31. Dordrecht: Springer Science & Business Media.
Marshall, Ruth. 2009. *Political Spiritualities: The Pentecostal Revolution in Nigeria*. Chicago and London: University of Chicago Press.
Mattingly, Cheryl. 2014. "The Moral Perils of a Superstrong Black Mother." *Ethos* 42(1): 119–138.
McDougall, Debra. 2009. "Christianity, Relationality and the Material Limits of Individualism: Reflections on Robbins's Becoming Sinners." *The Asia Pacific Journal of Anthropology* 10(1): 1–19.
Peletz, Michael G. 1997. "'Ordinary Muslims' and Muslim Resurgents in Contemporary Malaysia: Notes on an Ambivalent Relationship." In *Islam in an Era of Nation-States: Politics and Religious Renewal in Muslim Southeast Asia*, ed. Robert W. Hefner and Patricia Horvatich, 231–273. Honolulu, HI: University of Hawai'i Press.
Pelkmans, Mathijs., ed. 2013a. *Ethnographies of Doubt: Faith and Uncertainty in Contemporary Societies*. New York: I.B. Tauris.
Pelkmans, Mathijs. 2013b. "Outline for an Ethnography of Doubt." In *Ethnographies of Doubt: Faith and Uncertainty in Contemporary Societies*, ed. Mathijs Pelkmans, 1–42. New York: I.B. Tauris.
Pype, Katrien. 2011. "Confession cum Deliverance: In/Dividuality of the Subject among Kinshasa's Born-Again Christians." *Journal of Religion in Africa* 41(3): 280–310.
Robbins, Joel. 2003. "What Is a Christian? Notes toward an Anthropology of Christianity." *Religion* 33(3): 191–199.
———. 2004. *Becoming Sinners: Christianity and Moral Torment in a Papua New Guinea Society*. Berkeley, CA: University of California Press.
———. 2007. "Continuity Thinking and the Problem of Christian Culture: Belief, Time, and the Anthropology of Christianity." *Current Anthropology* 48(1): 5–38.
———. 2014. "The Anthropology of Christianity: Unity, Diversity, New Directions: An Introduction to Supplement 10." *Current Anthropology* 55(S10): S157–S171.

Roy, Olivier. 1996. *The Failure of Political Islam*. Cambridge, MA: Harvard University Press.

Rudnyckyj, Daromir. 2010. *Spiritual Economies: Islam, Globalization, and the Afterlife of Development*. Ithaca, NY: Cornell University Press.

Schielke, Samuli. 2010. "Second Thoughts about the Anthropology of Islam, or How to Make Sense of Grand Schemes in Everyday Life." Berlin: Zentrum Moderner Orient Working Papers, no. 2.

———. 2015. *Egypt in the Future Tense: Hope, Frustration, and Ambivalence Before and After 2011*. Bloomington, IN: Indiana University Press.

Schielke, Samuli, and Liza Debevec, eds. 2012. *Ordinary Lives and Grand Schemes: An Anthropology of Everyday Religion*. New York and Oxford: Berghahn Books.

Scott, Michael W. 2005. "'I Was Like Abraham': Notes on the Anthropology of Christianity from the Solomon Islands." *Ethnos* 70(1): 101–125.

Simon, Gregory M. 2014. *Caged in on the Outside: Moral Subjectivity, Selfhood, and Islam in Minangkabau, Indonesia*. Honolulu, HI: University of Hawai'i Press.

Soares, Benjamin., ed. 2006. *Muslim-Christian Encounters in Africa*. Leiden: Brill.

Soares, Benjamin, and Filippo Osella. 2009. "Islam, Politics, Anthropology." *Journal of the Royal Anthropological Institute* 15(S1): S1–S23.

Starrett, Gregory. 1998. *Putting Islam to Work: Education, Politics, and Religious Transformation in Egypt*. Berkeley, CA: University of California Press.

Strhan, Anna. 2015. *Aliens and Strangers? The Struggle for Coherence in the Everyday Lives of Evangelicals*. Oxford: Oxford University Press.

Sykes, Karen., ed. 2008. *Ethnographies of Moral Reasoning: Living Paradoxes of a Global Age*. London and New York: Palgrave Macmillan.

Throop, C. Jason. 2010. *Suffering and Sentiment: Exploring the Vicissitudes of Experience and Pain in Yap*. Berkeley, CA: University of California Press.

Tomlinson, Matt, and Matthew E. Engelke. 2006. "Meaning, Anthropology, Christianity." In *The Limits of Meaning: Case Studies in the Anthropology of Christianity*, ed. Matthew Engelke and Matt Tomlinson, 1–37. New York and Oxford: Berghahn Books.

Turner, Bryan S., ed. 2008. "Special Issue: Piety, Politics and Islam." *Contemporary Islam* 2(1).

Van der Veer, Peter. 2008. "Embodiment, Materiality, and Power: A Review Essay." *Comparative Studies in Society and History* 50(3): 809–818.

Verkaaik, Oskar. 2014. "The Art of Imperfection: Contemporary Synagogues in Germany and the Netherlands." *Journal of the Royal Anthropological Institute* 20(3): 486–504.

Zigon, Jarrett. 2008. *Morality: An Anthropological Perspective*. New York: Berg.

Chapter 1

IN WHAT DOES FAILURE SUCCEED?
Conceptions of Sin and the Role of Human Moral
Vulnerability in Pentecostal and Charismatic Christianity

Joel Robbins and Leanne Williams Green

The idea of original sin puts the likelihood of certain kinds of failure at the very heart of the Christian religious tradition. In many branches of this tradition, humans are in part defined by their initial failure to heed God's word and they are destined as a result to wrestle with their susceptibility to moral failure throughout the span of their earthly existence as a species. This susceptibility to failure is not a contingent fact about human beings, nor is it due to a mistake or oversight in how the cosmos is put together. It is part of how things are and are supposed to be. Without it, Christianity would not have the shape it has; it would not define salvation in the ways it does nor would it make salvation central to its definition of religious purpose. Put otherwise, whatever else human failure may be in Christianity—a disappointment, a curse, a source of frustration—it is also motivating, both of the nature of Christianity as a religion and of the ways many believers live their lives. And as motivating, it has positive results. As theologian Tatha Wiley (2002: 4) argues, the "idea of original sin first arose as an answer to … [the] question of redemption"—it explains the need for the figure of Christ and for the salvation he can provide. Thus the idea of original sin motivates people to seek salvation and it can lead God to show mercy; it can, in short, form the basis of the divine-human relationship.

Notes for this chapter begin on page 35.

Without human failure, this relationship would be without ground, or would be grounded differently than it is in many forms of Christianity as they currently exist. Against the background of the importance of sin in many kinds of Christianity, this chapter unfolds as an exploration of the complex and diverse understandings of human failure that exist in one strand of the Christian tradition. In terms of our understanding of religion, the chapter is an invitation to think about failure differently, to "reverse the sign" under which we think about failure and to give its positive force its due.

Of course, the idea of original sin has a complex history. It is widely agreed that it only took anything like its currently recognizable form in the work of Augustine in the fifth century CE and from that time forward there have been some differences in how various branches of Christianity have understood its nature (Wiley 2002; Jacobs 2008). So while many if not all forms of Christianity deal with issues of human failure through the lens of notions of original sin, they do not all do so in the same way. One could approach these differences by turning to the history of theology, and we draw on bits and pieces of that history here. But our main focus will not be on the elite theological tradition, but will rather be on contemporary ethnographic materials.

Even within the relatively narrow but by now ethnographically rich confines of the anthropological study of Pentecostal and charismatic Christianity, two distinct patterns of conceptualizing and reckoning with human failure are evident. In one, the blame for sin is placed squarely on the shoulders of the sinning individual. Sin is a personal problem that follows from an individual's failure to control themselves or to seek the good in the present by aligning their wills with that of God and must be dealt with by the person involved (with the support of their religious leaders and the members of the Trinity) in order to insure his or her salvation as well as to improve the quality of his or her life on earth. In this configuration, people sometimes seek such salvation through confession (frequently personal but also sometimes through the Church) and by praying to God for the strength to control themselves better in the future when they again face the temptations of sin. Sometimes other rituals, such as those of cleansing or reconciliation, are also available to aid people in their efforts to overcome the effect of sins they have committed. As we will discuss below, the Urapmin of Papua New Guinea exemplify this pattern.

The second configuration of human failure we consider looks quite different. In this pattern, best documented ethnographically among several charismatic Christian groups in various parts of sub-Saharan Africa, people's failures are closely tied to their possession or direction by evil spirits, and the opening that allows for the influence of these spirits tends to be rooted in a person's past, often in their upbringing in a religious system other than Christianity or in their continuing kinship relationships with people who practice such religions. Where failure is understood in these terms, the cause of people's problems is not solely their own in the way it is in the first pattern. Correlatively, even as individuals are still responsible for reckoning with their own situations, they do so primarily by seeking protection from spiritual attack or by practicing rituals of healing and deliverance, though they may also turn to confession. They may pray to God to strengthen their self-control, but much more often they pray to him for strength in their battle against the demonic forces that seek to control them against their own will.

The two patterns of thinking about human sinfulness we explore in ethnographic terms here are not recent developments. As Alan Jacobs (2008: 95) puts it, whether humans are driven to sin "from the inside out or the outside in" has long been a subject of debate in Christian theology. Augustine himself focused on individual problems of unruly desire. But even before Augustine stabilized the Christian focus on original sin, Justin Martyr, writing in the second century CE, explained the role of evil in human life by noting that there are "malign demons ... swarming everything, they have obsessed men's souls and bodies, infecting them with vices and corruption" (quoted in Wiley 2002: 44). We are thus using contemporary materials to explore anthropologically a very old pattern of variation in Christian understandings of sin. The ultimate goal of our argument is both to document the existence in contemporary ethnographic materials of these two understandings of human sinfulness and to explore the ways that, even as both of them put human failure at the very center of their concern, they put failure to religious use in different ways.

On Internal Sources of Sin among the Urapmin of Papua New Guinea

Joel Robbins carried out fieldwork among the Urapmin of Papua New Guinea in the early 1990s. He has discussed the importance of ideas about sin in the Urapmin experience of Christianity in some detail in the past (Robbins 2004a). Here, however, we isolate Urapmin thinking about the sources of sin within the human person and consider how this thinking influences their understanding of Christianity more broadly.

The Urapmin are a language group of approximately four hundred people living in the West Sepik Province of Papua New Guinea. The region in which the Urapmin live was not colonized until after World War II, but by the early 1950s Australian Baptist Missionaries had arrived at the regional colonial headquarters of Telefomin. In light of the small size of the Urapmin population, and their distance from the mission station, Baptist missionaries never spent much time in Urapmin, only rarely passing through on reconnaissance patrols around the area. Yet the Urapmin were struck by the conversions going on amongst their neighbors with whom the missionaries had been working more consistently, and in the 1960s they sent a number of young people to the Baptist mission station at Telefomin to study the new religion. Many of these young people converted and they brought a basic understanding of Christianity back to the Urapmin community. But as youths lacking religious authority in their own community, they were unable to convert many of those who had stayed at home, so traditional Urapmin religion remained dominant in the community, even as knowledge of the tenets of Christianity became widespread. This religious configuration remained stable in Urapmin through the first half of the 1970s.

Then, in 1977, things changed dramatically. During that year, a charismatic revival movement swept through Papua New Guinea. It was carried from community to community by Papua New Guineans themselves. Several Urapmin men encountered the revival in the regional bush Bible College in which they were studying and quickly brought news of it back to Urapmin. Upon hearing about the revival, people in Urapmin began to pray it would come to them too and soon many people were being "kicked" by the Holy Spirit, a form of possession that led them to tremble violently, feel very hot, and experience a strong sense of their own sinfulness. As Urapmin narrate their own history, it was having such ecstatic experiences themselves, or watching their relatives have them, that led people to realize that the Christian God truly exists and to convert to Christianity in the hopes of achieving salvation in Christian terms. By the end of 1977, all adults and teenagers in Urapmin had become Christian and since that time the community has self-consciously defined itself as a completely Christian one.

The account we have just given of Urapmin conversion is a very compressed one (Robbins 2004a offers a more detailed history). But even in such an abbreviated discussion, one should note that it is impossible to leave out the topic of sin. As Urapmin tell the story of the revival, their initial experiences of possession by the Holy Spirit were important not only for convincing them of the existence of the Christian God, but also for bringing them to an understanding of their own sinfulness. From the start, then, for the Urapmin it was in part their understanding of their sinful nature as human beings, and their need to turn to God for help to address the problems of salvation this sinfulness raised, that propelled them toward conversion. The motivating power of the human propensity to moral failure is thus a crucial part of the story of their coming to Christianity. But how do they understand this propensity to fail?

If one looks at Urapmin understandings of the causes of sin in relation to the well-known literature on charismatic Christianity in sub-Saharan Africa that we will discuss later, one thing that stands out is how little a role the Devil plays in them. Urapmin do have a notion of the Devil (Debil,[1] Satan), but they do not much elaborate on this figure. Sometimes "Devil" almost seems like a genus name for a range of species of "bad spirits" *(sinik mafak)*. Moreover, the devil is not nearly as important in Urapmin thinking as traditional nature spirits *(motobil)*, which are the cause of most illnesses and which are a topic of constant concern and discussion in a way that the Devil is not (Robbins 2009). Most importantly for our purposes, people in Urapmin never talk about the Devil as a cause of sin, or as a figure that explains misfortunes that befall people as a result of their sins. For the Urapmin, sin is explicable wholly in terms of their rather gloomy Christian view of human moral psychology—there is no need to turn to forces outside the person to account for it—and sin itself is sufficient to explain many of the bad things that happen in the world.

At the center of Augustine's view of original sin stands the notion of concupiscence or disordered desire. Later Christian thought has been unsettled over the question of whether the disordered nature of human desire is in itself what should be called original sin or is rather the consequence of such sin (Wiley 2002: 95–96). But regardless of where different Christian traditions have come down on this question, many of them have figured concupiscence as the heart of the matter when it comes to explaining the human propensity for moral failure. The Urapmin belong in this company, for their Christian moral psychology reckons disordered desire as the primary obstacle faced by people trying to lead good Christian lives.

The Urapmin term we gloss as something close to concupiscence is one that translates in more familiar terms as "willfulness" *(futabemin)*. In Tok Pisin, this is sometimes referred to as "<u>bikhet</u>" (from English "big headedness") and it has the sense of following one's own desires without regard to the legitimate moral expectations of others or to the will of God. In order to fully understand the importance of willfulness in Urapmin thinking about sin, it is helpful to note that Urapmin moral psychology is built around conceptions of two primary faculties that exist in the human heart (*aget* – the seat for Urapmin of all thought, feeling, and motivation). The first of these faculties is what the Urapmin call the will *(san)*. This is the selfish part of the person—the part that wants what it wants and is willing to disregard or "push" (<u>pus</u>) others around in order to get it. It is often driven by feelings of anger *(aget atul)* and envy *(tiin lawut inin)*, though it sometimes manifests as nothing more than an overwhelming desire for something. People's hearts also house a second faculty the Urapmin call "good thinking" *(aget fukinin tangbal)*, one that lends them the capacity to recognize the need to pay attention to the desires of others and to regulate their own wills in accord with collectively recognized laws *(awem)* that govern good behavior *(kukup tangbal)*. In ways that need not detain us here, traditional Urapmin moral thought enjoins people to balance expressions of willfulness and the lawfulness that follows from good thinking in the course of their lives. In doing so, it gives the will important roles to play in the everyday drama of Urapmin existence, though it insists that the will also needs in many contexts to give way to promptings toward lawfulness that are also an important part of people's make up (for details on this traditional moral system, see Robbins 2004a).

Urapmin Christian understanding of the moral nature of the person differs significantly from the traditional one, though it too figures the will and the capacity to recognize the demands of the law as important features of the person. The key difference between Christian and traditional moral thought is that the Christian version does not encourage people to find ways of balancing willfulness and lawfulness, but instead defines all willfulness as sinful and identifies lawfulness with acting in accord with God's will. For Christian Urapmin, the primary moral struggle people must engage in thus consists in "suppressing" (<u>daunim</u>) their own wills so that their hearts are open to the promptings of God's demands. Success in this endeavor leaves one with a "calm" (<u>isi</u>) heart *(aget)* filled with good thinking. This is the state Urapmin claim leads one to be ready for salvation when Jesus returns.

But this state of calm is not an easy one to achieve. Urapmin most often refer to sin using the Tok Pisin term "<u>sin</u>", a straightforward loan from English.

On rare occasions one also hears them refer to sins as "pekatos," presumably from the Latin by way of Italian. But the Urap word for it is *yum*, a term which also means "debt." In line with major currents in Christian theology, Urapmin often say Jesus came to "buy us back" (baim bak yumi), figuring redemption as following from Jesus' settling of the debt of sin by his death. But even in the wake of this redemption, humans still struggle with their sinful nature. The human will still wants to go its own way. Moreover, as Robbins has discussed at great length elsewhere and so we will only assert here, Urapmin social life continues to require that people exercise their wills in ways that contravene the law and also the will of God (Robbins 2004a). For this reason, a state of ease and calm that signals that one is without sin is one the Urapmin find impossible to sustain. Most of the time, people in Urapmin feel themselves to be sinners. This felt sense of sinfulness deeply informs people's broader sense that human beings in general, or at least in Papua New Guinea (a point on which we cannot elaborate here, but see Robbins 2004a), are defined by their propensity to moral failure.

But the recognition of human moral weakness does not sap the Urapmin of religious or moral energy. It is, rather, something akin to the engine of their Christian ritual life.[2] Urapmin attend church services in order to listen to sermons that will "strengthen" their "belief" (strongim bilip) and thereby aid them in their struggle against sin. And inside and outside of church they routinely pray to God for his help in this effort. Further, they address the sins they do commit by resort to rituals of confession (autim sin). Urapmin treat confession as a very important rite, and they have developed a very Catholic-looking practice whereby people confess privately to pastors or deacons before undertaking dances (Spirit disko) in church aimed at removing residues of sin from the body and rendering participants ready for salvation. People keep track of their sins in memory—some younger people even keep written lists—and they approach confession and the dances that follow as the most solemn of Christian rites. It is only at the end of the paired confession and sin-removing rites that Urapmin feel confident that they know they are truly ready for salvation. Yet this feeling is fleeting. For as a Urapmin person once put it to Robbins, as soon as people leave the church after a dance, they will immediately start sinning again—an observation that gives eloquent voice to Urapmin views of the extent to which human beings are by nature sinful creatures.

Given their emphasis on human sinfulness, it should perhaps come as no surprise that the Urapmin reckon heaven—the place to which salvation gains a person entry—as a place without sin. Like many Christians, the Urapmin do not elaborate at great length on what heaven is like. But they are firm in their conviction that in heaven people have no desires, and therefore feel no willful promptings. Heaven is a place where everyone's heart is easy and where no one is driven to sin. It is not the Devil who is absent in heaven, or at least the Urapmin do not stress this point, but rather the disordered desires of the human heart. Just as people are driven to sin by their own human failings, so too the overcoming of sin is a matter of a reordering of the human heart, rather than the outcome of a battle between cosmic figures for sovereignty over human lives. It is not that in Urapmin conception God does not battle demons. They regularly, for example, ask him to vanquish the nature spirits who make them sick, but these battles are not the cause of—nor is their resolution the cure for—the sinfulness that inheres in the very make-up of the human heart. For many other Christians around the world, however, such cosmic battles play a much more central role in defining the nature of sin and in accounting for the moral situation in which human beings find themselves. It is to a discussion of this second kind of understanding that we now turn.

Sin and the Devil in Sub-Saharan Africa

The explosive growth of Pentecostal and neo-Pentecostal churches in sub-Saharan Africa has sometimes resulted in a very different understanding of human religious and moral failure than the one we have just examined from Papua New Guinea. In a number of cases, such failures are more often understood as following from demonic influence and temptation than as proceeding directly, without external prompting, from flaws in human character. Two ethnographic accounts evidencing this pattern of accounting for failure are Birgit Meyer's (1999) study of the European Protestant missionary encounter with Ewe in South East Ghana and Paul Gifford's (2004) description of the more recent neo-Pentecostal growth in the same region. These two cases demonstrate with great clarity the ways this second understanding differs from those that construe religious failure as caused predominantly by internal human weakness. At the same time, the cases themselves are complex, for they tell the story of how the internal and external understandings of human failure might coexist in the same religious setting, in these instances where missionaries that hoped to foster the largely internal understanding find themselves inadvertently setting the stage for the emergence of the external one.

Meyer's account details the arrival of German Pietist missionaries in South East Ghana in 1847 and focuses on the role that teachings about the Devil played in their proselytizing efforts. The pre-Christian Ewe cosmology was populated by a wealth of spirits, varying in size and degree of influence on human life. The Ewe petitioned these spirits through tangible activities, whether by ceremonial performance or through divination using animals and objects. When the German Pietists arrived and began preaching their evangelical message, they associated the traditional Ewe spirits with the Devil in their missionary rhetoric, and this association was subsequently adopted by new Ewe Christians themselves (1999: 103). As Meyer (ibid.: 84) puts it "The Devil was the link between the missionaries' and the Ewe's worldview: to state that Ewe religion was a work of Satan made it meaningful in the light of Christianity."

By contrast with the Urapmin case we described above, where the Devil did not figure significantly in people's reasoning about conversion, the Devil's power to influence vulnerable people was an important motivating factor in Ewe conversion to Christianity. Practitioners of Christianity in Ewe claimed access to a God who could compete with the various spirits in their cosmos, spirits who had been collapsed into one figure—the Christian Devil. Christianity also provided a reason and a means to break with the kinship practices and accompanying familial and social obligations that were tied closely with rituals directed toward Ewe spirit beings.

Though much of Meyer's work focuses on how the figure of the Devil became the point of intersection for religious exchange during the missionary period, this interaction is also closely tied to the account she gives for the later rise of Pentecostalism in the region. The demonic idiom through which Christianity was introduced set the terms for future disagreements between missionaries and Ewe Christians about the sites at which human failure or success were to be located, and these disagreements played an important part in instigating the growth of Pentecostal and charismatically oriented churches.

The history of Ewe engagement with Christianity bears on our discussion because the divisions that developed within Ghanaian churches, and subsequently spurred converts to develop new church congregations, sprang from differing conceptions of the best way to combat evil. The disagreements centered, that is to say, on which religious practices were the most effective at addressing the risks posed by human failure in Christian terms. Early Ewe converts joined the newly founded Evangelical Presbyterian Church (EPC), which was shaped decisively by the teachings of the German Pietists. But Pietist missionaries and Ewe Christians had different views about which Christian practices could or should protect humans from the vulnerabilities brought about by their sin. German Pietists saw evil in the world as rising from the "intrinsic sinfulness of human beings which made them give in to Satan's temptations" (1999: 85). They understood sin as a product of personal corruption and wrong desires, a view which fits most closely with the first conceptual pattern we described above. The EPC considered devotional discipline to be the main mode of protection offered to a Christian: pursue orderliness and diligence in your work and religious life, and you will keep the dangers of your own sinfulness in check. As a result, in their Pietism they emphasized the importance of remorse and "belief," rather than ritual approaches to dealing with God (ibid.: 76).

Though the Pietist missionaries had earlier devoted attention to the role of the Devil at work through Ewe traditional spirits, particularly as a way to convince Ewe to convert to Christianity, EPC leaders soon began to shun any overt focus on the role of external spiritual agents. The missionaries simultaneously expressed exasperation that Ghanaian converts seemed not to feel the depth of their human sinfulness. Missionaries viewed sin as an issue of personal and of internal failure, but most Ewe Christians saw sin as something "endured" as opposed to an act "committed by themselves" (1999: 102). They attributed evil to the activity of the Devil, and saw sin more generally as a worldly reality that they had to withstand: the Devil was the reason for "the existence of sickness and death, but also anti-social, immoral habits and behavior such as greediness" (ibid.: 41). Furthermore, converts were frustrated by the absence of Church ritual prophylaxis available to them to ward off such threats of evil from spiritual forces that they saw as still very active in their lives. Ewe were accustomed to participating in traditional ritual festivals and sacrifices, activities through which they could directly address cosmic spirits and the havoc those spirits could wreak on health, family, crops, or political relationships. The EPC condemned these rituals, instead guiding converts toward personal devotional practices. Ewe believers, however, were dissatisfied with the inadequacy of these devotional rites, seeing them as providing insufficient protection from the consequences of sin that existed in the world around them. Converts felt themselves to be lacking the tools that they needed to address the root of their human failure—that is, their vulnerability to still-powerful traditional Ewe spirits.

Meyer's work makes it clear that the alternatives of defining failure as an innately human problem versus attributing it to the power of external forces (demonic or generally cosmic) over humans produced a significant cleavage between the EPC and a growing group of Ewe converts. The result was the founding of two new churches in the latter half of the twentieth century: the EPC "of Ghana" and what came to be known as the Lord's Pentecostal Church. Both churches grew out of prayer groups, which were settings intended for the practice of Christian religious rituals of healing and deliverance, rather than the propagation of the doctrinal and moral orders that were the focus of EPC services. The new churches gave prominent roles to charismatic prophets, who had the important task of interpreting the nature of the spirits attacking people and then performing or prescribing healing rituals. Members of the Lord's Pentecostal Church emphasized the spiritual agency of the biblical text, as words through which the Holy Spirit worked, and promoted personal charismatic experience as the main channel for knowing God. Prophecy, prayer and healing gave the newer churches a way to directly engage the spiritual attacks that led them to experience various moral and physical failures.

For many Ewe Christians, the defenses provided by the activities of the EPC of Ghana and the Lord's Pentecostal Church offered the only effective solution to their vulnerability to spiritual attacks, attacks that often moved through family channels. While witchcraft *(adze)* was viewed as a real threat to the harmony of Ewe kin relationships (1999: 188), attending to clan spirits *(trɔwo)* worked to "unite and protect [the clan's] members" (ibid.: 179). But various ancestral spirits could also cause intermittent problems or misfortunes for family members, until the spirits were appropriately aided or pacified. Even after conversion, spirits could haunt a believer if their family members chose to persist in holding clan festivals to their *trɔ.*

As a case in point, one woman became an early member of the Lord's Pentecostal Church after her baby fell ill. It was determined that the illness of her daughter was ascribable to attack from an ancestral stool of the family, motivated in part by the ritual festivities of the woman's uncle on the day of the baby's birth. A chief from the clan was dying and his spirit was attempting to take the girl along with him in his death (1999: 182). The ancestral spirits "could not 'come upon'" the mother because of her "staunch church membership" but the baby was "not yet 'under' the protection of any spirit," leaving the child vulnerable to attack from the stool's spirit (ibid.: 182). The mother later acknowledged that the mission-founded EPC had "'no provisions for healing'" and "'did not know how to pray'" (1999: 183). Instead, she saw the prayers of the Pentecostal splinter group as effective in repelling the spirit's attack and achieving the child's eventual protection and healing.

The appeal of the EPC of Ghana and the Lord's Pentecostal Church, as opposed to the mission-founded EPC, is that they both "protect" and "cure" people from spirits, particularly those *trɔ* that plague members, for while "the Devil operates through blood ties, the Christian God severs them" (ibid.: 187). Those who become Christians disrupt the kinship ties that make worship of the clan *trɔ* an act of familial belonging, but it is the prayers of the Christian specialists in charismatic practice that defend the believer from the power that the Devil might wield over them by working through these very family lines.

Perhaps most revealing about Meyer's account is that it turns on interactions between those standing on either side of the division between the two broad ways Christians deal with failure that we have been discussing here. The missionary approach to the persisting spiritual concerns of their converts in Peel's account (2003) of the Yoruba of southwestern Nigeria also dwells on the same division between two views of the sources of human weakness and failure. In attempts to convert the Yoruba, English agents of the Church Missionary Society "drew upon a mix of European common sense, technological effects, and popular science to challenge the view that behind mundane phenomena lay a myriad of hidden forces" (Peel 2003: 260). Though Yoruba Christian converts would hand over idols in a visible display of their conversion, there remained a striking inconclusiveness on the part of the missionaries about the nature of Yoruba spirits. Peel notes that the missionaries themselves seemed unsure if they were supposed to view Yoruba spirits as active agents of the Devil, or as only a product of superstition. Yoruba Christians declared their idols and "old spirits" defeated, but missionaries preferred to locate threats from the Devil closer to home, in human choices and failings. Foreign church leaders in Peel's account worked to make the Devil real in "immanent, ethical terms," which differed significantly from the "external, physical [terms] in which Yoruba Christians were disposed to figure him" (ibid.: 263). Peel remarks on the resulting cleavage between missionary and Yoruba Christian views of evil: "[i]t is not surprising that people who found the evangelical tenet of humanity's intrinsic sinfulness so alien to their thinking should be drawn to a concept of evil as a spoiling, external force" (2003: 264).

Other reports of thriving sub-Saharan Pentecostal and neo-Pentecostal churches also pinpoint a focus on healing from and protection against attacks by demonic powers as key to these churches' identities and popularity. Paul Gifford's (2004) account of the new "faith gospel" churches booming in the urban centers of Ghana suggests something additional about how these Christians view their own religious goals and failures. The churches that Gifford surveys themselves represent a considerable range of divergent charismatic beliefs, partly as dynamic responses to successive forms of Christianity. Several of the reasons that Gifford gives for the attractiveness of some (but not all) of these neo-Pentecostal congregations to Ghanaian Christians are similar to those Meyer offers to explain the appeal of the EPC of Ghana and the Lord's Pentecostal Church to the Ewe. These newer churches offer ritual opportunities to fight spiritual evils that threaten people's health and progress in the world. Prayer, healing and teaching are all successful methods for allowing believers to pursue a life free of the potential "blockages" that might prevent their general success, whether that success be a thriving business, physical vitality, a large family, or good exam results (Gifford 2004: 89). Most often obstructions to success are presumed to be caused by malevolent spiritual agents—agents that are local, dynamic, demonic, and possess their own personalities.

In several of the churches that Gifford describes, the Christian is threatened by the presence of evil spirits in the world. But a believer's reliance on God's power, enacted through charismatic prophets and healers, can help to remove the spiritual agents that cause lust, envy, or reliance on "traditional" kinship rituals, which makes believers vulnerable to attack. When a business is unsuccessful, the owners and employees claim the prosperity that is rightfully theirs by ridding themselves and their activities of the demonic spirit that clearly plagues them. The goal is to overcome "blockages" toward a victorious life, but moral piety is not the main avenue to achieve this life, nor does it offer the most robust protection against malevolent agents. The believer's "victory"— that is, the opposite of human failure—is not cast in terms of "the possibility of living a sinless life" (Gifford 2004: 80). Rather, it is "spiritual forces that largely determine states and actions, and it is the role of the man of God, through his miraculous gifts, to reverse unpropitious situations" (ibid.: 109). Religious success comes from accessing the charismatic prophet's power to remove, through ritual, the spiritual agents preventing a Christian from thriving.

Meyer and Gifford argue similarly that Pentecostal churches in sub-Saharan Africa are popular in large part because they provide dynamic praxis for combatting evil spirits, spirits that the historic mission churches were inclined to ignore. Peel ethnographically crystalizes a dimension of these Christian divisions by showing how the Devil and his capabilities are conceptualized very differently depending on where the cause of human failure is located. The African and Papua New Guinean Christians that we have described are all religiously motivated in important respects by the danger posed by the human failure that is a prominent theme in their respective Christian understandings. Yet what they see as the nature of sin, and the failure it entails, is markedly divergent and results in distinct practices with which they attempt to address it. The Urapmin practice rituals that entreat God and the Holy Spirit to help them control the willfulness that is a fact of their nature as human beings, and they use possession and cleansing rituals to counteract the effects of the sins they do commit on their moral status in relation to salvation. The Yoruba, Ewe and other Ghanaian charismatics seek experiences of deliverance through prayer, and turn to the insights and power of prophets to produce healing, remove "blockages," and defend them in the spiritual battles they fight against demonic powers that attack them from outside of themselves. Ethnographically, we have shown that such differing views of the nature of human weakness, while both being religiously motivating, lead to distinct practices for dealing with the resulting failure.

Conclusion

Our primary goal in this chapter has been to document two Christian patterns of understanding the human susceptibility to moral failure and to explore in both conceptions how failure becomes a key motivation for distinct forms of religious practice. In some respects, we would be happy to leave our chapter here, having simply noted some important differences between bodies of material on relatively recent Pentecostal and charismatic converts that anthropologists have often treated as broadly similar. The fact that we have been able to make these differences evident by treating the topic of failure in detail is an indication, as are many other contributions to this volume, that failure is a subject that should not be a peripheral one for scholars of religion, but is rather one that often reveals a great deal both about religious motivation and about the shapes taken by various religious traditions. By way of conclusion, we want to make a few merely suggestive observations about three issues that arise from our account. These issues deal with the importance of hybrid models of sin that fall between the two patterns we have discussed; possible reasons why some Christian groups pick up one pattern or the other; and some issues of responsibility and freedom that one might explore as a next step along the lines of investigation we have tried to open up here.

Jon Bialecki (2012: 312) has recently argued that for anthropological purposes, Christianity is not characterized by substantial similarities between its various expressions, but rather by the recurring nature of the problems many of its versions find themselves treating in often quite different ways. In this chapter, we have suggested that whether to place the origins of sin and human failure within or outside of the person is one such problem with which many forms of Christianity wrestle. Our approach to exploring this issue ethnographically is by presenting evidence of the most widely divergent internal and external patterns of locating sin as we can find data to support. By doing this, we mean to make the stakes of this problem clear. We do not, however, mean to suggest that all versions of Christianity fall neatly into the expression of one of these patterns or the other. We have seen, for example, that in the Ewe and other sub-Saharan African cases missionaries have made the internal problem a focus, even as many of the postmissionary era Christians in the region have adopted versions of Pentecostalism in which the external pattern is predominant. One can also find cases, even within the Pentecostal tradition, where the two patterns appear in mixed forms.

One case that evidences such mixing is described by Jeanne Rey (2013) in her study of the deliverance practices of Pentecostal African migrants in Geneva. The rituals of deliverance that these Christians perform presume that the causes of people's wrongdoing is the result of spirits who enter their bodies from the outside and must be expelled. In Rey's example, two identifiable kinds of spirits cause problems related particularly to sexual infidelity or infertility. But while both men and women are haunted by the activities of these spirits, it is women who are possessed and then exorcised in "deliverance" rituals performed, notably, by male pastors. For these Christians, all humans are vulnerable to evil from the outside on the basis of their fundamental human weakness, but this plays out through strikingly gendered norms of responsibility. Women are implicated as co-conspirators in their own possession because the power of both kinds of spirit that Rey discusses draws from the "seductive" capabilities of women (ibid.: 70). While ultimately these "deliverance practices tend to forsake the idea of an individual responsibility for one's sexual behavior," women are still "largely held responsible" for male sexual misconduct (2013: 73–74). Those under attack are also held strongly responsible for their own spiritual vulnerability when pastors issue warnings to women about keeping the power of their own sexual attractiveness at bay, powers which are attributed to external spirits but are understood to be general attributes belonging to women. We briefly highlight this case to suggest one example where human failure is taken to be, simultaneously, the direct result of external spiritual forces and also of inherent and inescapable, but potentially controllable, personal attributes. In this instance, gendered norms surrounding responsibility and failure allow for a mixing of the two patterns that we have suggested exist in Pentecostal conceptions of the nature of human failure.

A second issue we want to raise in conclusion concerns asking how one might explain the fact that some groups take a more internal and some a more external view of the location of sin. There are many potential ways to approach this question. One might look for more sociological explanations of the kind developed by Mary Douglas (1970) in her book *Natural Symbols*, by means of which one could correlate different notions of group boundedness and the rule-governed nature of personal conduct with judgments of how open or closed the human body is held to be, and then relate these latter judgments to where people locate the most important sources of human sinfulness or failure. In more cultural and historical terms, by contrast, one could look at the influence of traditional cultural ideas in shaping how converts think about the sources of failure and sin. Peel hints at this in the passage quoted above in which he relates the absence of ideas of original sin in Yoruba traditional thought to the way converts emphasize the Devil and the demonic more generally as an external force of failure in their lives. Likewise, Robbins (2004a), in a previous discussion of Urapmin morality, notes that even before conversion the Urapmin tended to see moral life as involving a great deal of internal personal struggle. It would not be difficult to argue on the basis of this that the Urapmin would be likely to find internal accounts of the nature of sinfulness compelling by virtue of the broad congruence between such accounts and these earlier understandings of human moral difficulty. And in similar cultural and historical terms, a reviewer of this chapter helpfully suggested that the mixed nature of the case presented by Rey that we discussed above may follow from the diasporic situation she studies, in which one can imagine traditional and novel European models may well have been blended, and which could indicate that such mixing might occur in other settings where people experience significant social change or a confrontation of alternative models of responsibility (though for a case detailing a similar ethnographic phenomenon, but in a nondiasporic setting, see Van de Kamp 2011).

Still staying within the realm of cultural and historical analysis, one might also focus on changing trends in global Christian understandings of sin, rather than on traditional cultural ones, to account for the distribution of different patterns of accounting for sin. Along these lines, one thinks of Ruth Marshall's (2009) discussion of how Nigerian Christianity has moved from an earlier ascetic "holiness" phase to a latter "prosperity" one. This move tracks a broader global shift from a period in which what is sometimes now called "classical Pentecostalism" was growing very rapidly around the globe to one in which a form that is labeled "neo-Pentecostalism" has surpassed it in terms of growth (Synan [1971]1997; Robbins 2004b). For our purposes, what is most noteworthy about this shift is that ascetic forms of Pentecostalism tend to emphasize the internal pattern, while neo-Pentecostal ones almost invariably give prominence to the external one. The timing of Urapmin conversion puts them squarely in the period when the ascetic form of Pentecostalism was dominant in Melanesia, while the sub-Saharan African cases we have considered tend to be neo-Pentecostal in character. One could become even more fine-grained in the examination of the globalization of forms of Christianity, tracing internal and external patterns across various denominations and then looking at how they have been reproduced as each expression of Christianity has spread. On such an account, the internal emphasis of the Urapmin might also follow from the nature of the Baptist faith to which they were first exposed, a reformed strand of Christianity that often focuses on human fallenness (for an account of a Baptist conception of sin that is similar to the Urapmin one, but from a very different cultural setting, see Greenhouse 1986: 77). In similar terms, one could follow Gifford (2004) in tracking globally diffused historical trends in Ghanaian Pentecostalism, figuring the current emphasis on deliverance from evil spirits in some churches as a response to the failures of the earlier neo-Pentecostal prosperity gospel that only serves to deepen an already present focus on external causes of human failure, while the changing social, economic and political climate in Ghana has led a few charismatic "prophets" to seek to promote an opposed focus on internal moral culpability. But we will leave off considering cultural and historical explanations for the distribution of various conceptions of the location of sin at this point. The explanatory suggestions we have offered here are meant only to be suggestive of possible avenues for future work, not to be exhaustive either in relation to the cases we have discussed or more broadly.

We bring this chapter to a close with a few more merely suggestive remarks, this time focused on the topics of responsibility and freedom. In 1972, Max Gluckman published an important edited volume devoted to, as its title put the matter, "The Allocation of Responsibility." This book was dedicated to Evans-Pritchard and it is therefore noteworthy that a few years later Mary Douglas (1980) would publish a short book devoted to Evans-Pritchard suggesting that the unifying thread in his work was an enduring interest in issues of account-ability—the ways responsibility is fixed in the course of social life. Much more recently, James Laidlaw (2013) has moved to make issues of responsibility, along with those of culturally defined notions of freedom, central to the rap-idly developing anthropology of morality. One way to read our chapter is to see it as a contribution to such discussions of responsibility and freedom made from the point of view of failure (see also Van de Kamp, this volume). Failure, like misfortune in the work of Evans-Pritchard, inevitably raises issues of responsibility and freedom and the varied doctrines of the sources of sin we have examined are Christian efforts to address them. It is by bringing failure to account and then trying to address its causes and effects that religion makes failure motivating in the way we have sought to highlight, and at least in the cases we have discussed, Christian notions of failure also tie responsibility crucially to issues of freedom. Ethnographically, an important next step for the project we have embarked on here would be to focus on responsibility and allied notions of freedom directly, treating them as failure's perhaps unexpected siblings. We hope to have hinted at ways one might explore such themes in this light, even as we have not been able to pay them the attention we have paid to failure in this chapter.

Joel Robbins is Professor of Anthropology at the University of Cambridge. Much of his work has focused on the anthropological study of Christianity and of morality.

Leanne Williams Green is a Ph.D. candidate in the Department of Anthropology at the University of California, San Diego. Her dissertation research focuses on morality and social change in the lives of urban Baptists in Harare, Zimbabwe.

Notes

1. In this chapter, terms in the Urap language will be given in italics, while those in Tok Pisin, the most important lingua franca in Papua New Guinea and a language that is important for Urapmin Christianity, will be underlined.
2. In his contribution to this volume, Martijn de Koning similarly argues that the rec-ognition of moral weakness fuels ethical cultivation among Salafi Muslims in the Netherlands.

References

Bialecki, Jon. 2012. "Virtual Christianity in an Age of Nominalist Anthropology." *Anthropological Theory* 12(3): 295–319.

Douglas, Mary. 1970. *Natural Symbols: Explorations in Cosmology*. New York: Pantheon.
———. 1980. *Edward Evans-Pritchard: His Life, Work, Writings and Ideas*. New York: Viking.
Gifford, Paul. 2004. *Ghana's New Christianity: Pentecostalism in a Globalizing African Economy*. Bloomington, IN: Indiana University Press.
Greenhouse, Carol J. 1986. *Praying for Justice: Faith, Order, and Community in an American Town*. Ithaca, NY: Cornell University Press.
Jacobs, Alan. 2008. *Original Sin: A Cultural History*. New York: HarperOne.
Laidlaw, James. 2013. *The Subject of Virtue: An Anthropology of Ethics and Freedom*. Cambridge: Cambridge University Press.
Marshall, Ruth. 2009. *Political Spiritualities: The Pentecostal Revolution in Nigeria*. Chicago: University of Chicago Press.
Meyer, Birgit. 1999. *Translating the Devil: Religion and Modernity among the Ewe in Ghana*. Trenton, NJ: Africa World Press.
Peel, John David Yeadon. 2003. *Religious Encounter and the Making of the Yoruba*. Bloomington, IN: Indiana University Press.
Rey, Jeanne. 2013. "Mermaids and Spirit Spouses: Rituals as Technologies of Gender in Transnational African Pentecostal Spaces." *Religion and Gender* 3(1): 60–75.
Robbins, Joel. 2004a. *Becoming Sinners: Christianity and Moral Torment in a Papua New Guinea Society*. Berkeley, CA: University of California Press.
———. 2004b. "The Globalization of Pentecostal and Charismatic Christianity." *Annual Review of Anthropology* 33: 117–143.
———. 2009. "Conversion, Hierarchy, and Cultural Change: Value and Syncretism in the Globalization of Pentecostal and Charismatic Christianity." In *Hierarchy: Persistence and Transformation in Social Formations*, ed. Knut Rio and Olaf H. Smedal, 65–88. New York and Oxford: Berghahn Books.
Synan, Vinson. [1971] 1997. *The Holiness-Pentecostal Tradition: Charismatic Movements in the Twentieth Century*, 2nd ed. Grand Rapids, MI: Eerdmans.
Van de Kamp, Linda. 2011. "Converting the Spirit Spouse: The Violent Transformation of the Pentecostal Female Body in Maputo, Mozambique" *Ethnos* 76(4): 510–533.
Wiley, Tatha. 2002. *Original Sin: Origins, Developments, Contemporary Meanings*. New York: Paulist Press.

Chapter 2

"I'M A WEAK SERVANT"
The Question of Sincerity and the Cultivation of
Weakness in the Lives of Dutch Salafi Muslims

Martijn de Koning

"When you say that you have a weak iman, I hope you truly believe that. Someone who states such things, but does little effort to strengthen one's iman, there is surely doubt whether his words constitute sincere modesty. If he truly believes, his actions would prove it" (Faouzi).

In the quote above one of my interlocutors in my Salafism research relates *iman* (iman is best translated here as inner faith) to effort, modesty and sincerity in response to a question I posted on Facebook (most of my interlocutors have befriended me on Facebook). I asked why so many of the people I work with emphasize that they have the best religion in their conversations with me and amongst each other, yet at the same time also claim to be "weak servants" who suffer from having a "weak iman." This question came up after I attended a meeting in 2013 with Dutch converts to Islam and was traveling home with a few of them whom I knew from my Salafism research. We discussed how they saw themselves as Muslims practicing the "true" Islam denouncing other Muslims whom they perceived as following a diluted or "cultured" Islam. At the same time they presented themselves in these conversations as weak. Also in many other instances I noted that my Salafi Muslim interlocutors claim that Salafi Muslims are the only "true" Muslims there are:

Notes for this chapter begin on page 51.

uniting the correct knowledge, intention and practice in fulfilling their duty to demonstrate the correct level of dedication to, and worship of, the unique and one God. At the same time, however, they describe themselves online and offline as weak and failing. I wondered how the people I work with in my Salafism research related both viewpoints to each other and decided to ask the question mentioned above. The responses given by Faouzi and others prompted me to revisit the notes and interviews that I conducted when I examined how Salafi religiosity was characterized by its emphasis on struggle (De Koning 2013a, 2013b). I realized that the idea of failure (encompassing other notions such as weakness and inadequacy) is very much an innate part of Salafi religiosity.

This chapter fits in well with a trend in anthropological research that is focused on how people strive for pious perfection and cultivate a moral self (Mahmood 2005; Fadil 2009), but, at the same time, it includes and discusses the ambiguities that daily life presents (Schielke 2009; Schielke and Debevec 2012), the personal doubts and uncertainties felt by people (Pelkmans 2013a), and the failures and limits of meaning (Engelke and Tomlinson 2007; Bielo 2008).[1] A focus on failure, ambiguity and uncertainty tells us how people, in their quest to fashion a moral self and achieve pious perfection, are challenged and informed by the inconsistencies and complexities of life in a society that does not always appreciate their endeavors and can even regard it with suspicion (cf. Marsden 2005: 260–61). My argument here is not that Salafi doctrines are often ambiguous and contradictory in themselves (although they are) or that Salafi Muslims sometimes fail to transfer their pious ambitions into their daily lives (which they do), or that they have to make compromises (which they have to and do do). Instead I will argue, firstly, that failure and weakness are both inextricable parts of their religiosity and self-fashioning and, secondly, that this self-fashioning in relation to ideas of weakness is not solely an individual project but a social one in which weakness is constituted, expressed and validated in social interaction with others.

First I will briefly outline the Islamic trend of Salafism, its rise in the Netherlands, and the reactions to it in media and government policies; the latter, in particular, informs us to a certain extent how Salafi Muslims in the Netherlands understand their position in society. I will then discuss a development in the study of Salafism that focuses more on the social dimensions of the daily lives of Salafi Muslims. This is a useful shift but neglects the question of having and acquiring sincere *(ikhlas)* intentions. The understanding of sincerity among my interlocutors is closely related to the central tenets of their concept of failure and is translated through their understanding of what "weakness" is. I will analyze this in more detail under the following categories: the idea of a weak *umma*, a weak iman, and being a weak servant. In so doing, I will illustrate how the relationship between trying to maintain a "correct" Islamic lifestyle and the everyday concerns and temptations that can lead individuals astray results in Salafi Muslims fashioning and expressing themselves as weak servants of God.

Salafism in the Netherlands

The Salafi movement is a global Sunni Islamic movement that originated in Saudi Arabia. The name Salafism is taken from the term "pious forefathers" *(al-salaf al-salih)*, the first three generations of Muslims, who are regarded as exemplifying the correct way that all Muslims should live today in all spheres of life (De Koning, Wagemakers, and Becker 2014).

Through fatwas, courses, conferences and websites, this broad perspective is converted into more concrete moral ambitions. In order to realize the Salafi utopia, Muslims should eradicate all the influences that could dilute their notion of a "true" Islam. The only way to lead a pure and authentic life, and consequently inherit Paradise, is to return to the period of the Prophet Muhammad and his companions as described in the sources of Islam, the Qur'an and the hadith. According to the Salafis, all human activity should be based upon a strict and literal reading of these sources if it is to be legitimate or it could be condemned as *bid'a* (innovation) or worse *kufr* (disbelief) (Meijer 2009; De Koning, Wagemakers, and Becker 2014).

From 1985 onwards, Salafi networks built a strong presence in the Netherlands, developing into a movement focused on purity, personal authenticity, and social relevance (De Koning 2013c). Certainly after 2000, when they focused more and more on courses and lectures given in Dutch, their preachers began to attract large audiences in their own mosques but also in other Islamic centers throughout the country. Sometimes Salafi networks cooperate but there is also strong competition between them as to who can attract the most participants in their courses. Sometimes the relations between them are strained because of ideological differences; in particular, those related to whether one should get involved in politics or not and if one should be loyal to Muslim political leaders (De Koning 2013a: 21–24; cf. Wiktorowicz 2006, Linge and Bangstad 2015).

The events of 9/11, the murder of the writer and filmmaker Theo van Gogh in 2004, and the rise of anti-Islam politicians such as Wilders resulted in the growing securitization of Islam; a process by which the focus in media, politics and integration was placed almost entirely on Muslims and Islam (and in particular Salafi Islam) and their alleged threat to democracy and social cohesion (De Koning 2013a: 21–24; cf. De Graaf 2011).

This chapter is based upon research I have conducted in several different Dutch Salafi networks from 2007 onwards. I have spoken to, and followed (on and offline), 48 men and 15 women since 2007, most of whom were aged between 16 and 25 years old with Moroccan-Dutch backgrounds, but also including several native Dutch converts, and Turkish-Dutch and Somali-Dutch Muslims. Besides this group of 63 people, I met and observed about 100 people during courses, conferences and lectures held on Salafi networks. Observation, informal conversations (in real and virtual contexts) and face-to-face interviews with men and women supplied the material. Most of the interviews were conducted in informal settings. Working with Salafi women was more complicated than working with the men, given the strong value many women and men attach to gender segregation; most of the interviews and informal talk with women were done via email, chat programs, and Facebook chats.

In this chapter I will focus predominantly on my observations of meetings in mosques, of Facebook discussions, and PalTalk (a chat program) chats. I used Facebook and PalTalk as a way of connecting with interlocutors online and as an integral part of my field site (cf. Burrell 2009) where I could interact and observe the people I work with. It is important to take into consideration that when people are talking to one another on a chat site by writing text, their texts and online names determine their online identity. On Facebook one shows who one is in a similar way but also with visuals and by displaying one's friends. I found that my research participants often engaged in debates online that they would not take up offline; this was particularly evident in debates between men and women, as the offline segregation between men and women is much stricter than online.

Salafism and the Question of Failure

Much of the literature on Salafism in Europe focuses on the processes of radicalization among Muslims (e.g., Amghar 2007), its attraction to Muslim youth because of the compatibility of Salafi discourse with the search for religious identity among second-generation Muslims seeking "pure" religion (e.g., Hamid 2009), or on the contradictions between daily life and Salafi ideologies and the tensions and uncertainties that ensue (e.g., Adraoui 2009; Dumbe and Tayob 2011). A recent special issue of *Comparative Islamic Studies* contained several articles that focused on the social dimensions of Salafism; articles that attempt to show the empowering and transformative dimensions of Salafism and how this produces and informs solidarities and conflict. Sedgwick (2014) correctly notes that much of the literature on Salafism is focused on doctrines (but see, e.g., Gauvain 2012) and tends to neglect the social life of Salafis.

This chapter takes up Sedgewick's suggestion and reflects, to some extent, the concerns explained by Olsson (2014), Dogan (2014) and Mårtensson (2014) in that special issue of *CIS*. They all focus on Salafi Muslims in Scandinavia. Mårtensson focuses on how a particular organization toned down its Salafi outlook and rhetoric in order to be able to fulfill its commitment to civic participation and activism. Dogan (2014), in particular, devotes much attention to how Salafi Muslims, for example, try to "purify" their homes, getting rid of items (such as photographs, for example) that are considered un-Islamic and try to stay away from those elements in daily life that might threaten one's attempt to stay on the correct path of Islam. They reflect on their lives and try to filter out all the influences that could potentially damage their piety. Olsson (2014) also elaborates on the practices of Salafi Muslims discussing their self-marginalization and self-separation from mainstream Swedish society and its Muslims. All three articles convincingly show how Salafi Muslims attempt to influence and realize their ambition to purify their social environment.

These are very insightful articles that add an important dimension to the study of Salafism by analyzing how Salafi Muslims live their lives in an environment that sometimes appears to be at odds with their ambitions of becoming pious Muslims and their ideas about "purity." They do, however, exhibit a rather unproblematic view of daily life and the tensions and uncertainties that people experience. As I have already argued elsewhere (De Koning 2013a), the view that wider society and daily life is at odds with Islam is something that is being taught within Salafi circles by preachers and is also a message that they understand from media and policies that focus on Salafism. Several authors do note how Salafi Muslims try to sacralize daily life by turning every mundane action into a matter of worship (Dogan 2014; Poljarevic 2014; Svensson 2014), but they do not take into account what the failure to uphold their ambitions means for their self-fashioning as pious Muslims (on this point, see also Kloos and Beekers, this volume). Furthermore, if it is indeed the case that Salafism fosters empowerment, a sense of moral superiority, and protection (Dogan 2014; cf. Meijer 2009), why do Salafi Muslims so often present themselves as "weak servants"?

In this chapter I will delve into Salafi Muslims' concerns about the impact their daily lives have on their piety and explore how the idea of being weak is related to self-improvement. I will argue that this is not solely an individual project but a social one in which weakness is constituted, expressed and validated in social interaction with others, in particular during online conversations. Before going into that I have to briefly introduce the question of sincerity, as this informs and shapes the self-understanding of Salafi Muslims as being weak. Take for example the next question posed on Islamqa by a woman to a Salafi imam (and posted on a Dutch website):[2]

> I do not know what causes me slowing down in my steps (in gathering knowledge about Islam and disseminating it). Is it because I did not achieve sincerity towards Allah, or something else? This makes me very sad. It hurts me and prevents me from achieving my goals. If there is any advice, do not withhold it from me, because I urgently need it.

The advice given by Islamqa is for her to just get on fulfilling her ambitions, not to procrastinate, and to be sincere. Although many of my Salafi interlocutors stressed the importance of having correctly sincere *(ikhlas)* intentions *(niya)*—for example, when going to prayer, going to school, or studying the Qur'an—it is not enough to simply have the correct intentions as many of my interlocutors and also preachers state.

A brief note about the way I use "intention" and "intentionality" is useful here. There has been considerable debate within anthropology and other disciplines on the matter of intentionality (cf. Robbins and Rumsey 2008). In particular Duranti (2015) has done a lot of work and claims intentionality is less central in how people attribute meaning and responsibility than might be expected in many Western accounts on the topic. Duranti (2015) argues that, in some contexts, people focus more on the consequences of others' actions than on the initial ideas. What matters here is that I focus on how my inter-locutors use the idea of intentionality and subsequently how intentions and actions should be related according to them. For the people I work with in my Salafism research, intention refers to an internalized objective creating a unity between those objectives and one's words. This is very much as Trilling (1971) conceptualized sincerity in relation to Calvinist ideas. As Keane (2002: 74–76), elaborating the ideas of Trilling, explains, this idea of sincerity is strongly related to a Protestant religion and to modernity where a subject acts as the source of its own authority. Salafi preachers locate a similar idea of sincerity but also refer to it as something that goes beyond the interior state of a person alone. They attempt to frame sincerity firmly within Islamic traditions in much the same way as the scholars who are associated with the Islamic revival in Mahmood's (2005: 65, 146) research do. She explains that for participants in her research particular attitudes must accompany the performance of the ritual acts: sincerity, humility, virtuous fear, and awe (Mahmood 2005: 123). Furthermore, Mahmood points to something I will build upon here: for Mahmood's interlocutors the exteriorization of sincerity in outward behavior (she gives the example of weeping) is more than just the expression of an interior faith, but also a means of acquiring it. Keane (2002: 75) says something similar when he states that sincerity is interactive: "For in being sincere, I am not only producing words that are transparent to my interior states but am producing them for you; I am making myself (as an inner self) available for you in the form of external, publicly available expressions."

It is not only one's interior state that matters; sincerity has to be produced and made visible to others. For my interlocutors this externalization is necessary so that the individual and others know that he or she is being sincere in their faith. Sincerity is not something Salafi Muslims work on solely by themselves in their personal project to become a pious Muslim. The question of sincerity is shaped, informed and validated through social interactions. For Salafi Muslims sincerity is established and can be validated by themselves and others through clothing, language, having the correct circle of friends, and by behaving in an appropriate manner when dealing with others (in particular maintaining a separation between the sexes) (De Koning 2013c). For my interlocutors sincerity is strongly related to a sense of failure. In Salafism, with its emphasis on the purity of Islam and its enmity towards unbelief, a person must have the correct intentions, speak the truth and act and live the truth, according to the example set by the Prophet Muhammad and the first generations of Muslims. To be able to live as "good Muslims" who have their worldly desires under control and who are focused on obeying God, for many of my Salafi interlocutors, any ambiguities have to be redressed immediately. This differentiates them from other Muslims whom I have worked with in previous research who found the ambiguities of daily life in relation to Islam less problematic (De Koning 2008). For these individuals, dealing with the ambiguities and contradictions between moral standards and actual behavior does not necessarily lead to being less of a Muslim or a bad Muslim. For the Salafi Muslims, however, the failure of living up to these high moral standards means that one lacks conviction and seriousness and, therefore, also sincerity.

This means that the idea of sincerity is related to a sense of failure in at least three ways. First of all, in contrast to the Qur'an and the Prophet Muhammad, whose teachings are taken to be pure and absolute truths, the outside world is perceived as chaotic and messy. This is often emphasized by preachers in their lectures when they state that the world is in moral crisis precisely because people are not sincerely following the moral guidelines of Islam and because "infidels" are waging a "war against Islam." Secondly, if people do not follow these guidelines, they lack iman (inner faith). Although my Salafi interlocutors recognize that part of the essence of Salafi religiosity is struggle (De Koning 2013a), succumbing to the temptations of daily life (such as going to bars, hanging about and mixing with boys and girls, neglecting prayer) results in, and is the result of, a lack of sincerity. Thirdly, as they regard the Qur'an as perfect and the Prophet Muhammad as the perfect example for every Muslim to mold themselves on, contemporary Muslims can never achieve such a state of perfection. On the contrary, any claim to perfection is seen as the result of pride and arrogance, which nullifies all good deeds and therefore one's chances of entering Paradise. Being humble, therefore, is a way of showing one's sincerity. It is these three aspects that I will explore in more detail below. These aspects are not Salafi per se, or exclusively Muslim. In fact, they can remind us of similar experiences among Christian groups (Robbins 2004; Pype 2011). They are all related to an individual's sense of failure, or to the difficult struggle of living up to utopian ideals. For the Salafi Muslims in my research these struggles have to be grounded in what are considered the authentic sources of Islam; they also, at the same time, refer to and constitute different ways for Salafis to aspire to be "true" Muslims: be this as part of their umma, in their relationship with God or in fashioning themselves as pious Muslims.

"The Umma is Weak"

"The umma is weak, and some make it even weaker" is a quote from Abu Jandal, a member of a militant Salafi circle and now one of a group of Dutch foreign fighters in Syria. Although some practices of these groups (such as disturbing debates, spreading pro Al Qaeda propaganda, and traveling to Syria to join Jabhat al-Nusra and ISIS) are widely condemned by other Muslims (including Dutch Salafi Muslims), the sentiment he refers to here is shared widely among my Salafi interlocutors. Failure here has two locations: the outside world in general and the Muslim community in particular. The outside world is seen as chaotic, evil and tempting, which is something Schielke (2009) notes as well for Salafi Muslims. He shows, as I intend to demonstrate as well, that the idea of a perfect Islam and the experience of messy chaotic life reinforce each other.

The reactions among my interlocutors to this idea of a messy daily life range from an attempt to isolate oneself as a protection against the perceived negative influences of the world to proselytizing and trying to improve the image of Islam and to militant action. A few people feel that there is nothing they can do to change society and that it is better to shield oneself from the temptations of daily life. Or as Umm Safouane summarized it in a discussion in a chat room: "Dear brothers and sisters, wouldn't it be best not to get involved with questionable affairs, Insha Allaah?" The term "questionable affairs" here pertains to phenomena that are not in accordance with Islam, according to Umm Safouane. These phenomena could even lead people astray from what they see as the righteous path. In practice this means that one does not participate in Dutch society any more than is strictly necessary; for example, going to school (or sending their children to school, but preferably a state-funded Islamic school), work, buying food, and so on.

Others, however, feel the obligation to change society by *da'wa* (proselytizing). Although in most of the Salafi literature this usually refers to the practice of trying to convert others, in the context of the Dutch Islam debates, it also pertains to trying to change the negative image of Islam. So while the idea of external failure produces a need for isolation among some, others are mobilized to take action in a variety of ways. But often people subscribe to both a perceived need to isolate oneself and to participate and engage in action. Umm Safouane uses an explanation of the different types of actions that is based upon a hadith I have frequently encountered: "Whoever among you sees an evil action, let him change it with his hand; if he cannot, then with his tongue [by speaking out]; and if he cannot, then with his heart—and that is the weakest of faith."[3]

According to my respondents this means one has to take action against evil and, if that is not possible, one should speak out against it or, if that is also impossible, then one should hate it, which also means one must not engage with it. A verse from the Qur'an that is also often referred to is sura 3:10 which states: "You are the best nation produced [as an example] for mankind. You enjoin what is right and forbid what is wrong and believe in Allah. If only the People of the Scripture had believed, it would have been better for them. Among them are believers, but most of them are defiantly disobedient."

The preachers in the Salafi networks also often refer to the principle of "commanding good and forbidding evil," which is based upon the Qur'an verse mentioned above. They turn this principle against their own community, which is on the one hand the best community of all and at the same time consists of people who defy the will of God. In this way the principle becomes a means of purification and a call to Muslims to become obedient.

In this way Salafi preachers and other da'wa activists try to build and strengthen their claim to be the representatives of an uncompromising, eternal and universal truth that cannot and will not be adjusted to Dutch values. They argue instead that a return to the values of the early Muslims should be striven for, values that they idealize as central to an uncorrupted, pure Islamic religious community (De Koning 2013c).

Umm Safouane's reference to a hadith is important in itself here as well as the reference to the Qur'an verse. My research with Muslims outside the

Salafi circles (De Koning 2008) shows that the idea that the "true" Islam is to be found in the example of the first generation and the Qur'an and sunna is not exclusively Salafi. What distinguishes the Salafi Muslims I work with from many other Muslims in my research is the attempts of Salafi Muslims to firmly ground their convictions in the "correct" knowledge by directly referring to the Qur'an and hadith and as such providing "proof" *(dalil)* for their claims. The tension in the Qur'an verse 3:10 (mentioned above), which I have also often noted in my conversations with people, is between being the best community and yet having many defiant Muslims. This puts forward the idea that they have the duty to change things precisely because they are (or should be) the most exemplary Muslims. Furthermore, the idea of the weak umma also raises the perfect example: the glorified past of Islam. For the Salafi Muslims I work with this refers back not only to the early generations of Muslims but also to Andalusia during the times when Muslims ruled there. To the participants in my research this makes it clear that a Muslim's loyalty should be first and foremost with the umma; the fact that people do not behave in this way is a cause of the crisis in Muslim communities.

A lot of the criticism made by Salafi Muslims is not only leveled at Dutch and international political leaders who, according to them, are waging a war against Islam, but also to Muslim political leaders in the Middle East and to Islamic authorities in the Netherlands and the Middle East. Many Salafi Muslims believe that all these leaders are betraying Muslims and Muslim interests in order to preserve their friendly relations with the Western world or stay in favor with local government and maintain access to funding, which for many of the participants in my research, is a flagrant sign of "hypocrisy" and "insincerity." The idea that Muslims are divided and fighting wars against each other, as well as the toning down of Salafi leaders' speeches in many European countries in recent years, are seen as evidence of the deplorable state of the Muslim community. Those who remain critical of Muslim leaders and the Western world are, on the other hand, often called "sincere."

The way this critique works legitimizes the adoption of a careful da'wa approach. Although there are a few groups in the Netherlands making a plea for the implementation of Islamic laws, the majority of Salafi Muslims reject such a viewpoint (although they do share the ideal) by saying that Dutch society, in general, and Muslims, in particular, are not yet ready. Too many Muslims have gone astray so da'wa, therefore, should focus first and foremost upon returning Muslims to the righteous path instead of trying to plea for the implementation of Islamic laws. For a minority of my interlocutors, however, this is not enough. They fiercely criticize the fact that, in their view, Dutch Salafi authorities have toned down their rhetoric after the murder of Theo van Gogh in 2004. A minority also try to get involved in the public debate about Islam, but most Salafi factions shy away from politics, as they regard democracy as incompatible with Islam (De Koning 2013c).

An even smaller, but very vocal, faction within the Dutch Salafi communities also cites the authorities' inaction in response to the injustices caused by the invasions in Iraq and Afghanistan, and, more recently, the civil war in

Syria, where they blame President Assad for committing all kinds of atrocities. As it is (or at least was) relatively easy to reach the Syrian battlefields, the failure by Muslims and non-Muslims to act against Assad provides some Salafi men with the opportunity to take up what they regard as the most important duty for a Muslim: fighting for the sake of Allah. As Abu Muhammad explained to me "We have to do something! And what is better for a Muslim than [to] fight the cause of God and die in the process?"

Among their friends the Dutch fighters in Syria (certainly not all with a background in Salafi circles) are glorified as heroes who refuse to allow the global Muslim community to face injustice and humiliation. For the majority though, including most of the Dutch Salafi authorities, these men are tarnishing the image of Islam even more, as the different Islamic factions in Syria are suspected of committing war crimes. Nevertheless, Abu Muhammad's frustration that no one is helping the people in Syria is widely shared. The anger that is often the result of the perception of failure of the worldwide Muslim communities is rarely translated into violent action and can also produce acts of compassion and support; other Salafi networks have organized fundraisers and sent food, clothing and blankets to the Syrian people. The idea of failure can thus energize people to work even harder and inspire them to move beyond their habitual ideas, assumptions, truths, and practices (cf. Pelkmans 2013b).

Having a "Weak Iman"

While many of the explanations above refer to failure as something that is outside the individual or to something that they have no control over *(umma)*, a different reference places the responsibility for failure right back on the individual.[4] When the people I work with believe that they are sinning against Islam—for example, by having a boyfriend or girlfriend, or by dancing, listening to music, or neglecting the daily prayers—they say they are suffering from a "weak iman"; a weakened inner faith.

In some cases the tensions resulting from the demands of Salafism, secularism and pluralism can lead to (what has been called in Salafi circles) a "Salafi burn out": a sudden waning of religiosity after a period of intense practice (De Koning 2013c). While in the case of those suffering from a so-called Salafi burn out such a disorienting experience may result in apathy or in completely moving away from everything related to Islam, the idea of inadequacy can also lead to an even stronger commitment to Salafism. The best way to have an "iman boost" (as my informants call it) is to go to the lectures given by preachers and to be among friends, brothers and sisters, who move within the same Salafi circles. As I have observed while attending lectures and courses in the Salafi circles, preachers point their constituency to its own failures and to their lack of adherence to the ideals and the necessity of doing so. These meetings, therefore, add to the individual's experience of lacking iman and of getting a so-called iman boost (De Koning 2013a, 2013c).

A strong iman is necessary if one is to be able to withstand the predicaments of everyday life; predicaments that result not only from a moral crisis and the war against Islam, but which are also the product of living a life in luxury. As one of my interlocutors, Abu Said, told me: "This world has weakened us. We are used to a decent meal, a warm bed." According to Abu Said and others, the ease of daily life makes people forget about their duty to Islam and that they have God to thank for this. Also, when they see their peers with a different way of life they start getting doubts. Read, for example, the exchange between Umm Muhammad, Abu Nasr and Abu Omar in a chat room:

> Umm Muhammad: You know, I'm being really tested now with nice things, temptations, friends, you know … your friends from the old days.
> Abu Nasr: Subhannallah [Glorious is God, God is free from evil].
> Abu Omar: Those temptations will also be there.
> Umm Muhammad: They go out, do nice things, boys … you know. I'm getting a little depressed because of it haha.
> Abu Nasr: Those things are ancient history for me.
> Umm Muhammad: I always said the same, Abu Nasr. But unfortunately … I have become so weak, I doubt whether I'm even a Muslim.
> Abu Nasr: Subhannallah.
> Abu Omar: A3udhu billah [seek protection from God against evil]. Find refuge with God and make du'a [du'a; supplications]. Ask God for guidance and protection. Do not say that you are not a Muslim anymore.
> Umm Muhammad: Yes, that is what I've always been doing and [or] so long already. But perhaps God does not want to lead me anymore. … I don't have doubts about Islam, not at all. But those temptations, are real man. I took off my khimar [headscarf that covers the body except the face], do not wear hijab, nothing.

Umm Muhammad is worried here that God does not want to lead her anymore and that her iman and steadfastness are so weakened she can hardly be called a Muslim anymore. She stresses that she does not have doubts about Islam, but that she is not strong enough to resist the temptations of doing things with her old friends, things she feels go against Islam. It is significant that the exchange mentioned here takes place in a chat room. It is not likely that a conversation like this would take place in an offline setting where the separation between men and women is much stronger. Furthermore, an online environment in which people are to some extent anonymous is much more comfortable for talking about one's doubts and uncertainties and touching upon difficult issues (cf. Becker 2013).

As Liberatore (2013: 235–36) explains in relation to British Somali Muslims in London who had just started practicing Islam, the expression "weak iman" (or "low iman" as her interlocutors call it) provides people with an acceptable way of expressing doubts, uncertainties and inconsistencies between knowledge, intention, and behavior. Similarly, the Salafi Muslims in my research did not express their doubts, fears and uncertainties as such, but usually explained that they were suffering from a weak iman as a result of the predicaments and temptations of daily life. Furthermore, by using this language, the individuals concerned stay within the boundaries of Islam, confirming that no doubts exist about Islam itself. This type of language also, I suggest, enables people to share their concerns and problems without going into any great details about them. Umm Muhammad mentions the "temptations" but does not explain what they are, except by referring to, for example, "boys … you know." She appears to expect that others will understand and recognize what she is referring to anyway. Through use of this type of language, and within this online environment, Umm Muhammad is able to share her concerns with her chat room friends, who, in turn, express their understanding and support. A spiritual intimacy is created through interaction between people who recognize Umm Muhammad's concerns and who feel that they are in the same boat.

Talking about her concerns with others is a demonstration of Umm Muhammad's reflexive self, and it is these others who help her to establish guidelines about how to think of oneself. Sharing their suffering about having a weak iman also helps them to learn that they are not alone in this, that it is, in fact, normal and part of being a practicing Muslim (see also Liberatore 2013).

"I'm a Weak Servant"

Umm Isa: "We people have been created as weak."

Now we have seen how the participants in my research look upon the Muslim community as failing and often talk about themselves as suffering from a "weak iman" we can conclude that the idea of weakness is an intrinsic part of their self-fashioning as pious Muslims. There is more to it, however, because the former does not immediately explain why ideas pertaining to weakness are discussed so often in public, although within certain limits, as we have seen above.

According to many of my respondents, they realize that they will only find peace if they focus their mind on the superior God; man is weak but still the center of his creation. People can choose but if they choose the wrong things the mind will revolt. As I already explained in the introduction of this chapter, after having observed many discussions about the weakness of man, of the Muslim and of the umma, I decided to ask, on Facebook, why people are so proud to be part of the righteous path yet understand themselves as weak people who are failing to live up to Islam. Most of the reactions repeated the different ontologies I have explored above, but the next reaction by Umm Fatima added a layer I have not yet discussed but which I have often come across both in online and offline conversations:

> The Islamic creed as taught by the Prophet salla-llaahu 3alayhi wa-sallam [Peace be upon Him], the companions and the salaf, is taken as the absolute truth. This truth also consists of the idea that man is created weak and therefore makes mistakes.

Umm Fatima distinguishes here between an "authentic" Islam and people who are weak. The "authentic" Islam is beyond questioning; it is the absolute truth. The pious perfection people look for is located in the example of the Prophet Muhammad, his companions and the two generations of Muslims that follow. Although an individual may often express pride in being part of Islam or the global Muslim community and following the example of the first generations of Muslims, pride about one's piety is strongly disapproved of. Moreover, if a person shows off, this is generally seen as a lack of sincerity; one is striving for the approval of fellow Muslims, but a truly pious Muslim only wants and needs God's approval and satisfaction. In this way, expressing oneself as a weak servant struggling to gain God's satisfaction is therefore not only used as a legitimization for one's failures and as an imperative for developing oneself, it is also the public display of sincerity, showing one is striving for God's approval and never realizing it.

The public display of weakness reveals an interesting tension in the beliefs and practices of my informants. On the one hand it makes them appear to be pious and steadfast Muslims to outsiders (albeit these outsiders sometimes perceive them as arrogant and prideful as well), yet their self-identification with being weak and with being Muslims with weak iman also makes it clear that they are not living up to the ideals and ambitions of pious perfection. This tension is increased even further, as the public sharing of sin is highly disapproved of as well. This does not mean that people should not ask for forgiveness when they have done something or someone wrong, or not admit their sins, but there is a strong belief among my interlocutors that they should keep quiet about their sin, as it is nothing to be proud of. The Salafi Muslims in my research are therefore walking a thin line between refraining from publicly talking about one's sins and the public display of weakness. The latter, however, is approved of when it is combined with a struggle for God's approval. In the previous section we saw Abu Nasr replying to Umm Muhammad's statements about her uncertainties by urging her to seek refuge with God and ask Him for support. Also in my conversation with Umm Fatima presented here we can find something similar. In her response to my question mentioned above, she continued:

> The perfection of man is not in acting without faults, but in struggling to gain God's satisfaction whereby one remorsefully returns to God, in case of a particular mishap.
>
> This fact [that satisfaction is located in trying to gain God's approval and satisfaction] brings about a number of advantages of which only God knows the full extent. Such as a stronger relationship between servant and Lord, protecting oneself against the tricks of Shaytaan (devil) because you reflect about your mistakes, to abhor wrong and love good because you are aware of the fact that the sin has harmed you, and much more.

The state of weakness here gains a virtuous moral value; realizing one is weak is an important step in becoming a pious Muslim. It works as an imperative to become more pious and it is piety in itself that deepens the relationship one has with God. A state of weakness pertains to a lack of moral strength in one's relationship with God. It means that a Muslim has both the capacity and the duty to become a better Muslim. Being weak, therefore, is not the issue; on the contrary, it is neglecting one's duty to become stronger that is the problem.[5]

When presenting oneself as a weak servant, people are not just referring to their sins, they are discussing and displaying their efforts to become better Muslims whilst acknowledging they are weak servants. It is a statement about one's intentions as well as about one's actions and the consequences thereof. The emphasis on clothing, the frequent use of Arabic phrases among my interlocutors and presenting oneself as a weak servant all make visible the effort one is putting into monitoring and fashioning a moral self and trying to become a steadfast Muslim.

Conclusion

To become a pious Muslim is a continuous project for most of my interlocutors. The production of a pious Muslim subject, and its constant reconstruction, is the result of an attempt to ground one's convictions and actions in the written sources of Islam (Qur'an and hadith) and provide proof *(dalil)* of that. In doing so, having the correct, sincere intentions is crucial for the people I work with: without such intentions every act of worshipping God is useless (cf. Kloos, this volume). A failure to uphold their ambitions of becoming pious Muslims is taken to be a sign of insincerity and leads to self-doubt about one's sincerity in relation to God.

The idea and experiences of failure among my interlocutors are not only the result of tensions between Salafi doctrines and everyday reality, but are very much part of the lived experience of Salafi Muslims, or lived Salafism if you like. The public display of weakness and failure reveals an interesting paradox in Salafi religiosity among my interlocutors and provides us with some insight as to how Salafi Muslims define intentionality. It is important for them to have correctly sincere intentions but, to be recognized and valid, these intentions have to be made visible by sharing them with others in particular ways so that the individual and those around him/her know that he or she is sincere in his/her faith. Sincerity is thus produced and reproduced by sharing one's failures and weaknesses (and the attempts to redress them) with others who recognize it and support the person's efforts to become a pious Muslim and have a moral self. Furthermore, failure and weakness work as incentives to improve one's moral self and the surrounding world but do not determine the action itself. For example, the experience of the world facing a crisis and of the war against Islam can be translated into people isolating themselves, turning to charity, or engaging in violent action.

The public manifestation of people as weak servants also serves as a reminder and as an instrument against arrogance and pride (which would nullify the impression they wish to create as people with correct, sincere intentions) and renders visible their effort to become steadfast Muslims rather than a claim to actual perfection.

The perceived tension among Salafi Muslims between the ambition of achieving a state of perfect Islam and the sense of failure experienced in daily life is an important constituent element of lived Salafism. The idea of being a weak servant, of appreciating the idea of a perfect Islam, the sense of failure that arises from the ambition of perfection and the perception of a messy and tempting daily life are produced and reproduced through Salafi teachings and sharing one's concerns with others. The imperative to improve oneself gains significance through concerns they have with the challenges of everyday life and is constituted and reconstituted through social interaction with others.

Martijn de Koning trained as an anthropologist and works at the University of Amsterdam as a postdoctoral researcher for the NWO funded project "Forces that Bind or Divide" on Muslim interventions in the Dutch public sphere since 1989. He has published on the identity construction of Moroccan-Dutch youth, Salafi Muslims in the Netherlands, radicalization of Muslim youth, and the Dutch Islam debate. He teaches courses on the Middle East and on Islam in Europe at Radboud University Nijmegen.

Notes

1. See the introduction to this volume by Kloos and Beekers for a more elaborate discussion of the body of literature focusing on pious self-fashioning and that focusing on the ambiguities of daily life.
2. "Oprecht zijn tegenover Allah [Being sincere to Allah]." Retrieved 15 October 2014 from http://www.al-yaqeen.com/va/vraag.php?id = 1645
3. Narrated by Muslim, 49. Umm Safouane told me she got the hadith from the website Islamqa.com: http://islamqa.info/en/10081. Retrieved 2 November 2014.
4. On the relationship between failure and responsibility, see also the contributions in this volume by Robbins and Williams Green, Kloos, and Van de Kamp.
5. See Kloos, this volume, for a rather different understanding of the moral imperative of self-improvement among Muslims in Aceh, Indonesia.

References

Adraoui, Mohammed-Ali. 2009. "Salafism in France: Ideology, Practices and Contradictions." In *Global Salafism. Islam's New Religious Movement*, ed. Roel Meijer, 364–384. London: Hurst.

Amghar, Samir. 2007. "Salafism and Radicalisation of Young European Muslims." In *European Islam: Challenges for Public Policy and Society*, ed. Samir Boubekeur, Amel

Boubekeur, and Michael Emerson, 38–51. Brussels: Centre for European Policy Studies.

Becker, Carmen. 2013. "Learning to Be Authentic: Religious Practices of German and Dutch Muslims Following the Salafiyya in Forums and Chat Rooms." Nijmegen: Ph.D. dissertation. Radboud University.

Bielo, James. 2008. "On the Failure of 'Meaning': Bible Reading in the Anthropology of Christianity." *Culture and Religion* 9(1): 1–21.

Burrell, Jenna. 2009. "The Field Site as a Network: A Strategy for Locating Ethnographic Research." *Field Methods* 21(2): 181–199.

De Graaf, Beatrice. 2011 "Religion bites: Religieuze orthodoxie op de nationale Veiligheidsagenda." *Tijdschrift voor Religie, Recht en Beleid* 2(2): 62–80.

De Koning, Martijn. 2008. *Zoeken naar een zuivere islam: Geloofsbeleving en identiteitsvorming van jonge Marokkaans-Nederlandse moslims*. Amsterdam: Bert Bakker.

———. 2013a. "Between the Prophet and Paradise: The Salafi struggle in the Netherlands." *Canadian Journal of Netherlandic Studies* 33/34(2/1): 17–34.

———. 2013b. "How Should I Live as a 'True' Muslim? Regimes of Living among Dutch Muslims in the Salafi Movement." *Etnofoor* 25(2): 53–72.

———. 2013c. "The Moral Maze: Dutch Salafis and the Construction of a Moral Community of the Faithful." *Contemporary Islam* 7(1): 71–83.

De Koning, Martijn, Joas Wagemakers, and Carmen Becker. 2014. *Salafisme–Utopische idealen in een weerbarstige praktijk*. Almere: Uitgeverij Parthenon.

Dogan, Güney. 2014. "Moral Geographies and the Disciplining of Senses among Swedish Salafis." *Comparative Islamic Studies* 8(1–2): 93–112.

Dumbe, Yunus, and Abdulkader Tayob. 2011. "Salafis in Cape Town in Search of Purity, Certainty and Social Impact." *Die Welt des Islams* 51(2): 188–209.

Duranti, Alessandro. 2015. *The Anthropology of Intentions: Language in a World of Others*. Cambridge: Cambridge University Press.

Engelke, M., and M. Tomlinson, eds. 2007. *The Limits of Meaning: Case Studies in the Anthropology of Christianity*. New York and Oxford: Berghahn Books.

Fadil, Nadia. 2009. "Managing Affects and Sensibilities: The Case of Not-Handshaking and Not-Fasting." *Social Anthropology* 17(4): 439–454.

Gauvain, Richard. 2012. *Salafi Ritual Purity: In the Presence of God*. London and New York: Routledge.

Hamid, Sadek. 2009. "The Attraction of 'Authentic Islam': Salafism and British Muslim Youth." In *Global Salafism: Islam's New Religious Movement*, ed. Roel Meijer, 384–404. London: Hurst.

Keane, Webb. 2002. "Sincerity, 'Modernity,' and the Protestants." *Cultural Anthropology* 17(1): 65–92.

Liberatore, Giulia. 2013. "Doubt as a Double-Edged Sword: Unanswerable Questions and Practical Solutions among Newly Practising Somali Muslims in London." In *Ethnographies of Doubt: Faith and Uncertainty in Contemporary Societies*, ed. Mathijs Pelkmans, 225–251. London and New York: I.B. Tauris.

Linge, Marius, and Sindre Bangstad. 2015. "'Da'wa is Our Identity'—Salafism and IslamNet's Rationales for Action in a Norwegian Context." *Journal of Muslims in Europe* 4(2): 174–196.

Mahmood, Saba. 2005. *Politics of Piety: The Islamic Revival and the Feminist Subject*. Princeton: Princeton University Press.

Marsden, Magnus. 2005. *Living Islam: Muslim Religious Experience in Pakistan's North West Frontier*. Cambridge: Cambridge University Press.

Mårtensson, Ulrika. 2014. "Norwegian Ḥarakī Salafism: 'The Saved Sect' Hugs the Infidels." *Comparative Islamic Studies* 8 (1–2): 113–168.

Meijer, Roel. 2009. "Introduction: Genealogies of Salafism." In *Global Salafism: Islam's New Religious Movement*, ed. Roel Meijer, 1–32. London: Hurst.

Olsson, Susanne. 2014. "Swedish Puritan Salafism: A Hijra Within." *Comparative Islamic Studies* 8(1–2): 71–92.

Pelkmans, Mathijs. 2013a. *Ethnographies of Doubt: Faith and Uncertainty in Contemporary Societies*. London and New York: I.B. Tauris.

———. 2013b. "Outline for an Ethnography of Doubt." In *Ethnographies of Doubt: Faith and Uncertainty in Contemporary Societies*, ed. Mathijs Pelkmans, 1–42. London and New York: I.B. Tauris.

Poljarevic, Emin. 2014. "In Pursuit of Authenticity: Becoming a Salafi." *Comparative Islamic Studies* 8(1–2): 139–164.

Pype, Katrien. 2011. "Confession cum Deliverance: In/Dividuality of the Subject among Kinshasa's Born-Again Christians." *Journal of Religion in Africa* 41(3): 280–310.

Robbins, Joel. 2004. *Becoming Sinners: Christianity and Moral Torment in a Papua New Guinea Society*. Berkeley, CA: University of California Press.

Robbins, Joel, and Alan Rumsey. 2008. "Introduction: Cultural and Linguistic Anthropology and the Opacity of Other Minds." *Anthropological Quarterly* 81(2): 407–420.

Schielke, Samuli. 2009. "Being Good in Ramadan: Ambivalence, Fragmentation, and the Moral Self in the Lives of Young Egyptians." *Journal of the Royal Anthropological Institute* 15(1): 24–40.

Schielke, S., and L. Debevec. 2012. *Ordinary Lives and Grand Schemes: An Anthropology of Everyday Religion*. New York and Oxford: Berghahn Books.

Sedgwick, Mark. 2014. "Introduction: Salafism, the Social, and the Global Resurgence of Religion." *Comparative Islamic Studies* 8(1–2): 57–70.

Svensson, Jonas. 2014. "Mind the Beard! Deference, Purity and Islamization of Everyday Life as Micro-factors in a Salafi Cultural Epidemiology." *Comparative Islamic Studies* 8(1–2): 185–210.

Trilling, Lionel. 1971. *Sincerity and Authenticity*. Cambridge, MA: Harvard University.

Wiktorowicz, Quintan. 2006. "Anatomy of the Salafi Movement." *Studies in Conflict & Terrorism* 29(3): 207–239.

Chapter 3

SUCCESS, RISK, AND FAILURE
The Brazilian Prosperity Gospel in Mozambique

Linda van de Kamp

In November 2005, the biannual Campaign Fogueira Santa de Israel (Holy Bonfire of Israel, Fogueira for short) was launched by the pastors of the Brazilian neo-Pentecostal Universal Church of the Kingdom of God in Mozambique's capital city Maputo.[1] A huge sanctuary was built on the podium of every branch of the church in the city.[2] The sanctuary resembled the holiest place in the Jewish temple, as described in the Bible's Old Testament, where only priests were allowed to enter under special conditions to sacrifice an animal. A ladder to heaven was placed in the sanctuary, similar to the Old Testament's story of the ladder in Jacob's dream, which reached from earth to heaven.[3] While angels ascended and descended the ladder, God promised Jacob that through his seed all the families on earth would be blessed. To be part of this blessing, Mozambican believers who actively participated in the two-month long daily and nightly prayers, fasting, and money-saving for their special sacrifice *(sacrifício)* would be allowed to enter the holy place on the pulpit to present their sacrifice to God by placing it on the ladder: the sacrifice being a specially designed Campaign envelope filled with a very large amount of money, often a month's salary or even more.[4] Many participants sold their car or their house to sacrifice *(sacrificar)* money in church. According to the pastors, their courageous faith would be abundantly blessed. They would become successful entrepreneurs and find a loving partner.

Over the past decades, Pentecostalism has grown exponentially around the world (Anderson 2013). The present expansion of Pentecostalism in Mozambique, as in other places in Africa, has neo-Pentecostal features. Neo-Pentecostalism is known for its "Prosperity Gospel," emphasizing that it is God's will for believers to be rich, healthy and successful (Coleman 2000; Gifford 2004; Ukah 2005).[5] Following a divine logic of "sowing and reaping", believers' investments in both spiritual and monetary terms are believed to generate success for them in this world in the form of a prosperous life. Yet, during my periods of fieldwork in Mozambique from 2005 through 2011, I witnessed how various Pentecostal believers, rather than seeing their prosperity and happiness increase, experienced downward socioeconomic mobility and an unhappy family life as a result of their participation in Campaigns like the Fogueira. The aim of this chapter is to examine how Pentecostal Christians in Maputo incorporate the strong focus on "intelligent faith" in the churches, or the need to be responsible and rational in the realization of happy marriages and successful businesses, particularly when they fail to meet the neo-Pentecostal ethics of prosperity.

Addressing Mozambican believers' incorporation in their lives of the Prosperity Gospel can provide a valuable addition to our current insights on religion and well-being in the anthropology of Christianity and the sociology of religion more generally. Scholars have described how confronted with unfulfilled expectations for prosperity combined with the ascription of supernatural origins to the seemingly spectral wealth of the neoliberal economy, people in the Global South fervently adopt the Prosperity Gospel, attempting that way to likewise access health and wealth through powerful supernatural means (Comaroff and Comaroff 2000; Pfeiffer, Gimbel-Sherr, and Augusto 2007). Another prominent interpretation focuses on the role Pentecostal religion plays in advancing people's socioeconomic conditions and in bringing about personal transformation and empowerment (Berger 2009; Martin 2002; Attanasi and Yong 2012); for example, Pentecostalism teaches the attitudes and skills necessary for modern economic development, such as self-worth and entrepreneurship.[6] While these perspectives have helped us to better understand the attraction of the Prosperity Gospel, they cannot explain its popularity among people who do not consider global capitalism unsettling. Pentecostal believers in Mozambique are often upwardly mobile people actively engaging in the neoliberal economy by working in private companies, starting up (small) businesses, and making a profit. They are not looking for a safe shelter from which to judge the influences of the market economy; they are part of it.[7] Also, existing interpretations disregard the fact that engagement in the Prosperity Gospel can result in downward mobility.

As I will argue, the neo-Pentecostal ethical self-formation in Mozambique stimulates attitudes of calculated risk-taking to varying degrees, according to the understanding of risk as the inherent outcome of a conscious decision in which agents take into consideration that things might go wrong as opposed to hazards that occur without conscious human agency (Luhmann 1993; see also Bloemertz et al. 2012; Boholm 2003)—of the latter Pentecostals in Maputo accuse non-Pentecostal fellow Mozambicans, who would mainly be reacting to threats instead of planning their future life. As Lambek (2000: 316–17) observes in his discussion of religion and morality, Pentecostal practices in Mozambique provide occasions for believers to acknowledge their agency and commit themselves to bearing responsibility for their actions. This is so particularly, as I will demonstrate, when they fail to perform rightly.[8] Moreover, the particular form of Pentecostal responsibility that has been evolving in Maputo shows that Brazilian Pentecostalism there is part of the neoliberal order rather than being a response to it (see also Meyer 2007; Comaroff 2009).[9] Pentecostal believers learn to reframe sociomoral concerns from within a market rationality that requires people to be responsible in every domain of life, willingly bearing the consequences of their actions (Van Dijk 2010), and fitting the neoliberal principle of self-regulation (Shamir 2008).

The crucial point here is that, in the ethical model of the Brazilian Prosperity Gospel, failure in terms of achieving worldly prosperity means moral-religious failure, and vice versa. When my interlocutors in Mozambique experienced failure in worldly matters, such as business or their love life, their initial reaction was to regard this as a sign that they should be more determinate in their faith and, consequentially, invest more in the church. In other words: they were morally failing because they were not showing "intelligent faith" and taking enough calculated risks, seemingly acting without clear intentions and looking like those whose lives seem a continuous response to threats. There was, however, a tipping point. At some point, worldly failure would become so great that further escalation in terms of religious (monetary) investments was simply impossible (because they ran out of money or their enterprises went bankrupt). In some cases, this resulted in changing churches, as a way to relieve the pressure. In other cases—and it is this intriguing phenomenon I will be concentrating on in this chapter—more radical action was required. In such cases, my interlocutors turned to the possibility of modifying the ethical model of the Brazilian Prosperity Gospel altogether, by relating worldly failure to a lack of personal responsibility, rather than religious sincerity. In Mozambique, these personal transformations add up to a rather broad shift in the Brazilian Pentecostal movement, in which "intelligent faith" emerges as a new modality of dealing with the ever-present threats of moral failure in an environment in which Pentecostalism has taken on an increasingly "neoliberal" character, by reinforcing its very focus on personal responsibility.

My analysis is based on ethnographic research in the city of Maputo, where most of the Brazilian Pentecostal churches are based, and includes formal and informal interviews with sixty Pentecostal believers. After outlining some of the particular discourses of the Brazilian Prosperity Gospel in Mozambique, I will first turn my attention to the different ways in which two young Pentecostal women navigated the moral dilemmas arising in their lives in relation to changing responsibilities in the sphere of the family and amorous relationships. I will subsequently illustrate the eagerness of older Pentecostal women, participating in Pentecostal business courses to become part of the neoliberal socioeconomic order in Maputo. Having demonstrated how the neo-Pentecostal ethical formation of "taking responsibility" can involve different experiences of failure and success for both younger and older believers, I discuss in the conclusion why framing this Pentecostal self-formation as a process of calculated risk-taking rather than in terms of coping is an important point of inquiry allowing us to come to a better understanding of why exactly the Prosperity Gospel has become so popular in today's world. [10]

Brazilian Pentecostalism and "Intelligent Faith" in Mozambique

Pentecostalism is relatively new to Mozambique, where before independence from Portugal in 1975 the religious landscape was largely defined by traditional African religions, Islam, Catholicism, classic Protestantism, and African Independent Churches. In the postcolonial era, however, Evangelicals and Pentecostals are of growing importance, and according to the last census (INE 2010) they now represent 11 percent of the total population and 21 percent in the capital of Maputo.[11] This rapid growth is embodied in the new churches that have come from Brazil and that have sprung up in every neighborhood in Maputo and have come to define the face of neo-Pentecostalism in the urban areas (Cruz e Silva 2003; Freston 2005). The most visible Brazilian Pentecostal church is the Universal Church, followed by the Igreja Mundial do Poder de Deus (World Church of the Power of God) and Deus é Amor (God is Love). These churches appeared at the time market discourses were finding inroads in different spheres of Mozambican society. As observed by Lima (2007) for Brazil, there appears to be a correlation between the increasing spread of neoliberal discourses about entrepreneurship, the market and self-reliance in Mozambique and the growing popularity of Brazilian Pentecostalism, which fervently propagates the Prosperity Gospel.

The Brazilian version of the Prosperity Gospel in Mozambique has certain specific characteristics: its South South transnational features (Van de Kamp and Van Dijk 2010) are enhancing the efforts at pushing change and self-responsibility in converts' lives. In general, neo-Pentecostals assume that evil powers, often located in cultural traditions (Meyer 1998; see also Robbins and Williams Green, this volume), lie at the root of poverty and failure and have to be defeated. Explaining why people must break with demonic cultural traditions, Brazilian Pentecostal pastors denounce Afro-Brazilian religions as witchcraft. Since the religions of the African slaves (who were shipped to Brazil in the transatlantic past) form the basis of all kinds of Afro-Brazilian worship in Brazil, Brazilian pastors consider Africa as the original home of "evil spirits" (Macedo 2000). It is this evil that they have come to Africa to fight and this translates into a fierce combat against ancestral practices and cultural customs. Mozambican Pentecostals are thus exposed to Brazilian Pentecostalism's critical perspective on "African culture." The supposed close connection of "black" Brazilian pastors to "Africa" combined with their simultaneous position as outsiders appears to shape a particular relationship between Mozambican Pentecostals and Brazilian pastors (van de Kamp 2013a). In the Brazilian Pentecostal domain, ideal spouses can be found and businesses can be set up as a result of the new space that Brazilian pastors offer, moved away as they have from their past life, their families and their Afro-Brazilian religion, enabling them to offer Mozambicans the option to do the same (see also Mariz 2009). One has to transcend the familiar, one's family and culture, and suffer hardship to create new possibilities. The powerful atmosphere of conquest that Brazilian Pentecostalism consequently creates (Van de Kamp 2013a) is important in understanding the formations of Pentecostal moral actions in Maputo.

Through their participation in church activities and their engagement with (Afro-) Brazilian leaders, believers come to realize that through the boundless power of the Holy Spirit they can take responsibility for their own lives. The Afro-Brazilian Pentecostal push to break with evil "African" powers that cause misfortune requires people to demonstrate a radical change in behavior. This change often takes the form of a restructuring of family structures, novel forms of marriage, and new practices of doing business (see also Van Dijk 2012). Thus, for example, young Pentecostals told me how they enjoyed the openness about sexual matters among Brazilian pastors and how it helped them to look more critically at common "African" cultural patterns of sexual behavior in their society (Van de Kamp 2013b). It led some of them to contest the usual marriage arrangements, such as *lobolo* (bride price), by celebrating a Christian lobolo instead, in which the pastor takes on the role previously played by elderly kin. For these believers their new stance on (ancestral) kin and marriage are important in establishing a new ethical self that stresses one's personal responsibility to prosper in life as opposed to finding wealth in (kin) relations (cf. Ferguson 2013). This places a high level of moral responsibility on the individual believer to realize God's purpose for a prosperous life, which becomes very clear in the financial domain. The Pentecostal leaders organize business courses in which they continuously stress that believers should explore the market, "take ownership" *(tomar posse)*, "have courage" *(ter coragem)*, and be prepared to "take risks" *(tomar risco)*. As God is on the side of real believers, they will be successful. As a consequence, lack of success is seen as being the result of a lack of faith, as I will demonstrate below.

It was precisely because so many Pentecostals were not successful in their businesses and in their relationships that the main leader of the Universal Church, Brazil-based bishop Edir Macedo, introduced the concept of *fé inteligente* or intelligent faith. Special messages from the bishop, explaining the concept, were shown on screens during church services in Maputo. Much like the discourses I heard during the services, Macedo writes the following in one of his blogs:

> The inability to distinguish between what is emotional and what is spiritual has disastrous effects on Christian life. ... Emotional worship is based on emotions, nothing else. People cry, make promises of love and give in to emotional faith moved by appealing songs. In the adoration in spirit, our intellect works

in accordance with the Word of God. ... The use of rational faith involves two things: sincere recognition of God's greatness and *the demand* of His promises.[12] (italics added)

According to Macedo, people will only prosper if they are conscious of the spiritual acts of faith that they are required to perform to bring this about. His rationalist message of spiritual self-development is not very common in Pentecostalist circles and often seems to be at odds with the reliance on spontaneous divine intervention generally propagated (see also de Witte 2011). While Macedo may have coined this quite unique concept of intelligent faith, related discourses about responsible faith have been central elements in other Brazilian Pentecostal churches in Maputo as well. These discourses underscore the necessity of people realizing what faith entails, namely that divine intervention can only be expected when people show dedication and plan their life goals. It is within this framework that the leaders of the Universal Church put particular stress on believers knowing what they are doing when they sacrifice large amounts of money. If they do not, their sacrifice will not take them very far. People should not try "to make God a fool" by not seriously engaging in Campaigns like the Fogueira—their sacrifice should be a real sacrifice, giving money they cannot really do without and this should be a determined decision.

The Pentecostals I met often stressed how their attitudes of intelligent faith were opposed to the behavior of fellow citizens. For example, Paula (aged 37), who worked at a telecommunications company and frequented the Universal Church, said that she saw many people who were just *desenrascando* (from the verb *desenrascar*, which may be translated as "muddling through" (Vigh 2009: 424)):

> People are just sitting the whole day selling bananas and waiting for a job, but they have to do something. It is important to look forward. I have a good job and a good salary but I want to earn more money, so I'm always looking around for another job. You can't ask God and do nothing yourself.

In Maputo, people regularly mentioned the act of *desenrascar* as a form of getting the best of difficult socioeconomic situations and possibilities by using informal social and personal relations and resources.[13] While desenrascar can be approached as "the ability to envision one's way through emergent and volatile sociopolitical circumstances as well as being the actual practice of doing so" (Vigh 2009: 424), Pentecostals found this type of life strategy small-minded, as it did not sufficiently "test God." Brazilian Pentecostal pastors teach that every believer must "demand God's promises" (see Macedo above) by their actions of faith, most notably by excessive financial sacrifices to achieve "great things." Converts who give coins would receive coins in return; thus, these are worthless, said the pastors. To excel, converts are told, one should give banknotes, preferably in U.S. dollars, the currency that entrepreneurs use, and which is worth far more than Mozambican currency. Competition is encouraged among the congregation for quantities of money. During church services, the pastors call forward those who would give U.S.$500, then those who would give U.S.$300, and then U.S.$100, and so on. During the special *campanhas* (campaigns), such as the Fogueira, believers can test God even more by giving everything they have and more than that "to gain the right to collect their blessings." For Paula and other converts the point is that one must gain a competitive position in the market economy instead of just envisioning one's success, even if at high personal cost, as this proves how determined one is.

Challenges of Upward Mobility

Most people attending Brazilian neo-Pentecostal churches in Maputo are relatively successful socioeconomically and/or aspire to be and stay upwardly mobile in terms of education, career, and lifestyle. Normally, believers will at least have had a few years of elementary education and many of them have studied at institutes of higher education. The majority of these Pentecostals are women. These women have benefited from the new possibilities for socioeconomic mobility that came with the transition from a socialist-oriented economy to a neoliberal market economy as a result of the structural adjustment programs (see Pitcher 2002 for an overview). The reforms have made it possible for more women to enter the workforce or to create informal jobs (Sheldon 2002: 229–66). In line with their increasing socioeconomic independence, upwardly mobile women have been critically viewing cultural traditions in their society, where responsibility implies things like showing your dependence on kin. As in other places in Africa (e.g., Meyer 1998; Frahm-Arp 2010; Van Dijk 2012), these women are enthusiastic about the Pentecostal message of empowerment that calls on them to break with their dependencies on kin and to take initiative in building their professional careers in a competitive setting where there are not enough well-paid jobs to accommodate the growing group of educated people.[14]

Despite the new possibilities offered by the politics of privatization (Pitcher 2002), upwardly mobile people are experiencing constraints. A central concern is the extent to which one's income should be shared with one's respective families. The demands of extended families on the relatively wealthy upwardly mobile are experienced as a burden by the latter, who complain about the problems of setting up businesses and advancing because they need to take care of poorer relatives. Furthermore, young women in particular have difficulties finding a partner, as quite some men are afraid that these women (can) earn more than they do and that they will lose their position of influence (Manuel 2011: 154).[15] In addition, the rising consumerist desires and styles that often mark upward social mobility are increasingly marking marriage arrangements, as marriage celebrations have become an important status-marker for which the younger generation have become fully responsible in financial terms, while only a few can afford the enormous expense involved in getting married (Manuel 2011: 185–87). Because the Brazilian pastors explicitly address these tensions, many young upwardly mobile people have started to attend Pentecostal church services and counseling sessions on "planning your marriage" and "the real reason behind your relationship problems." In what follows, I will demonstrate how two young Pentecostal women incorporated Pentecostal ideals of prosperity with respect to marriage, and how they dealt with "successes" and "failures."

Realizing the Future

Elena and Marta, two young Pentecostal women in their early twenties, studied at university and were very ambitious.[16] They enthusiastically talked about how, in contrast to the gerontocratic power structures in their society, neo-Pentecostalism encouraged them to take initiative. Marta said: "I learned that when you have faith, you are really able to achieve something in your life." Elena had been an active member of the Universal Church for some years when I first met her. She frequented the special sessions in this church on love and marriage, where she met her boyfriend after receiving a spiritual revelation during a moment of prayer. However, she and her partner were each other's opposite in everything, and they developed a very complicated relationship. Her mother disapproved of their relationship. "But, we had faith. God had brought us together and we made plans about marrying and the future," Elena said. She was self-assured and began to dominate her boyfriend; they quarreled a lot. This happened in the same period that the church's leadership started preaching about intelligent faith. Elena said it made her realize that "it is not only faith [i.e., emotional faith], you have to use your brains as well." She decided to break up with her boyfriend and to take more time to learn to embody "real faith"—that is, intelligent faith.

Looking back, Elena felt that her enthusiasm for the Pentecostal emphasis on self-responsibility had been mainly based on her emotional reaction after the spiritual revelation she had had in church. She now stressed the importance of both "listening to the Holy Spirit," who could, for example, speak through the pastors' words, and of taking personal responsibility by not stopping to rationally judge her situation. Interestingly, she therefore also sensed that she should take the advice of her elders, such as her mother, more seriously, even if this went against what the pastors propagated. Elena thus tried to strike a balance between acting independently and listening to her elders, to pastors, and the Holy Spirit, particularly where her relationships with men were concerned. Her emotional sense of failure turned out to be fruitful in her Pentecostal self-transformation, as she learned that a sign of the Holy Spirit is not enough. What she felt was required was an entire transformation of one's being and acting, including not disregarding one's rationality, that would make her a good and productive Christian (see also Campos and Gusmão 2008).

The ambiguities in Elena's experiences with regard to balancing personal responsibility with the power of different authorities also transpires in Marta's account, but with a different outcome. Marta had frequented different Brazilian Pentecostal churches since she was seventeen, the Universal Church being one of them, and when I first met her she was frequenting the Maná church.[17] Marta and her boyfriend were saving up money for their wedding. Every time I talked to Marta her marriage was just around the corner. Difficulties emerged when the respective families demanded that a long list of relatives were to be invited for the marriage celebrations. Following the Pentecostal teachings on financial planning and careful decision-making when starting a family, Marta and her boyfriend, who was also a Pentecostal, had decided to economize on their wedding by not inviting too many people. They were aware that this meant that their marriage would be less prestigious in the eyes of friends and relatives, but they had plans for building a house and starting a business. Although they did not give in to all the demands, they were nevertheless forced to change their plans and had to postpone their marriage by a few years due to a lack of financial resources. Marta's studies took much longer than originally planned and the business they started was not as successful as they had hoped.

Marta felt that her responsible faith was continuously being tested, not only by her kin but also by the pastors. During the years they were planning their marriage, Marta's pastors often warned her that she should come to church more often. She always explained to her pastor that she needed the time to study even if she loved the thought of going to church more often. But according to the pastor she should "first seek God's kingdom and all other things would be given to her as well," following a Bible verse in Matthew 6. The pastor confronted her with the fact that she had failed a number of exams and that she was still not married. In Marta's view she would not be showing intelligent faith if all the time she were to ask God for success while at the same time neglecting her studies—studying naturally leading to success—much like the sermon in which the pastor stated: "How can one ask God for a car, but not take driving lessons?" After another year in which she felt that the pastor was only putting pressure on her instead of also listening to her rational motives of faith, she and her boyfriend moved to another Brazilian Pentecostal church.

What is striking in the accounts of Elena and Marta is that intelligent faith can at the same time be part of the Pentecostal project of self-transformation and become a vehicle of criticism against it; particularly against the interpretation of it by most Pentecostal pastors. It appears that what many Pentecostal leaders consider to be intelligent faith is focused on one's performances in the church, such as attending the daily services. Believers like Marta and Elena, however, are more concerned with developing the right faith by making their faith productive at university and in their relationships, meaning that they cannot comply with all the pastor's demands. Against this backdrop, acquiring religious perfection as described by Mahmood in her study of the women's mosque movement in Egypt (2005) does not necessarily imply the constant performance of all the required religious formats to develop one's ethical self. What also counts for these young Pentecostals is the moral reasoning behind how to balance their multiple and conflicting responsibilities, judging how to live their lives wisely in the face of the various challenges presenting themselves (Lambek 2000: 314–15). Believers like Marta and Elena are working on a relationship with God in which the Pentecostal discourse matches their aspirations to take responsibility in their lives, and instead of simply accepting Pentecostal obligations transforming these by their actions. This also implies that when believers feel that the pastor's words of advice do not prepare them well enough for the challenges they are facing, they move on to get better spiritual guidance in a new church. This seemed to work differently for older Pentecostals, such as the ones I met during a business course.

"Managers of the Nation's Wealth"

The Universal Church's business course "Managers of the Nation's Wealth" consisted of ten weekly lessons given by pastors. The course was meant for converts with a business or plans to start one, and the central message was that course participants should "think big." God gave the nations, and thus the world, to his managers—that is, to the course participants, if they were willing to show their faith. The pastors taught the rationality of the market based on the Gospel; for example, by using Jesus's parables on sowing and reaping (see also Gifford 2004: 44–82). The participants were encouraged if not pushed into becoming entrepreneurs by taking risks and exploring the unfamiliar (see also Van Dijk 2010, 2012). They were challenged to act in the neoliberal market economy, taking the initiative to set up as many businesses as possible because God detests poverty and wants to bless abundantly. Converts had to write business plans, set goals, pray for divine inspiration, and sacrifice money.

The participants of the course that I attended were almost all women aged between forty and sixty.[18] They were very eager to participate in the market economy, such as the three friends Maria, Silmara, and Isabel, all in their late fifties and followers of Brazilian Pentecostalism since the early 1990s. They stressed how the pastors had encouraged them to pursue professional careers. Maria considered the years she had worked in a factory as a waste of time, because she could have been studying. During her childhood, she had never attended school regularly and her father had sent her to work in a factory in Maputo in the 1960s, at the end of the colonial era (cf. Penvenne 1997). But now, in the neoliberal era, she and the other women were all keen to participate in the new socioeconomic order: they had taken up new studies and had set up several small businesses. They were busy living the Pentecostal spirit of taking initiative.

Isabel always emphasized the struggle she was going through. Early in the morning she went to church, during the day she worked, and in the evenings she attended classes. There was no time to rest, because at the weekends she had to prepare for exams and check up on her businesses. She also had to visit her parents and resolve family conflicts. She tried not to become too deeply involved in family issues but her kin complained that she was not contributing enough financially. According to Isabel, everyone should be responsible for their own finances and she tried to pass on the pastors' lessons on individual responsibility to her kin. Having participated in numerous Campaigns of the Universal Church, Maria finally succeeded in being selected for a Master's program in Brazil. Silmara, however, was less successful.

The participants in the course had to present their business plans to the pastors in a private meeting. Silmara was uncertain about her plan and after the meeting she reported that the pastor had given her negative feedback. She had several small businesses but they were not expanding and the pastor made it clear that she had to change her strategies. In one session she had to demonstrate her commitment to becoming a prosperous manager by throwing grape juice (symbolizing Jesus's blood) over the pastor and telling him the amount of money she would sacrifice to reach the goal she had set. However, after having sacrificed for several years, she ran into difficulties with her business because she could not invest enough capital in it. When in the Fogueira Campaign that this chapter opened with, she sacrificed the remaining savings she had left and finally went bankrupt.[19] She was ashamed about her failure and did not want anybody to know about her situation. She did not even inform her children, even though for several months she barely had enough to eat, as she told me later. She was divorced and lived alone.

I had expected that Silmara would be angry with the church and its pastors because of the pressure they put on her to sacrifice all her profits to the church, but I was surprised to hear that she was angry with herself instead. "How could I have been so blind?" she asked. She started frequenting the Brazilian Pentecostal World Church of the Power of God—she had been a member of the Universal Church for fifteen years—"where I am learning facts I never knew." Thus, for example, she learned about the Apostle Peter, who writes about false teachers who in their greed will make a profit out of telling you made-up stories (2 Peter 2). "In the Universal Church they were selective in quoting Bible texts," Silmara stated. While she was critical about the behavior of some of the pastors at the Universal Church, she continued to blame herself. She could have read the Bible passages she was learning about in the new church. In line with the idea of intelligent faith, she had not used her brains but instead "I submitted myself to their pressure" because she was afraid she would not be performing her faith correctly. Thus instead of intelligent faith she had demonstrated emotional faith.

According to Maria and Isabel, who no longer spoke to Silmara since she left the Universal Church but guessed what had happened, Silmara had indeed not used her faith intelligently. Isabel said: "You must use intelligent faith. I don't feel obliged to always give what [the money] the pastors ask for. In the beginning, I did, as many did and do, but it isn't necessary. You have to give when you want to and are able to. Silmara was too obedient." Maria commented that when she participated in the Fogueira for the first time it did not work because she was not really committed:

> The Fogueira is not just something. For a long time, I didn't understand it, it isn't something anybody can do. You must really want to do it and not have any doubts, and then big things will happen. ... The first time I participated, oh I

was really innocent. I earned a salary of 1 million [about U.S.$30] each month, and I gave it with many requests, ... The other Fogueiras, I wasn't strong, I was doubtful, not serious, I was playing. But this year, I started things right. I now participate with a lot of faith. It is necessary to have a lot of faith. I feel that good things are going to happen.

When I asked a question about the time she was doubtful, she said, "look, I was just muddling through [*épá, estava só a desenrascar*]." She took a risk by giving her salary away, as she and her children depended on it for their daily survival, but had done so in an awaiting mode without a clear goal. But now, the risk she took would be rewarded, as she was dedicated and offered her money consciously during the Fogueira. Maria was one of the several converts I met who, with a great deal of effort, had been gradually successful. She managed, as she dearly wished, to get the scholarship to study abroad and had started to build a house.

For believers like Maria, Isabel and eventually also Silmara, sacrifices have become the way to demonstrate and confirm their new ethical self, showing that they are "eager, determined and know what they want," as the pastors often stress. Bataille described the sacrifice as a rupture, as "the necessity of throwing oneself or something of oneself out of the self" (in Elmer 2012: 86), eventually leading to the radical alteration of the person. Similarly, by sacrificing everything they have, Pentecostal believers materialize their new position in life, which effectively means that they abandon their social security networks. By offering their money in church, they disconnect themselves from local conceptions for achieving prosperity, such as sharing wealth with kin. This becomes visible in situations where Pentecostal sacrifices fuel distrust because of the denial of social obligations (see also Newell 2007), one reason why Silmara did not share the details of her financial situation with her children. Isabel felt how her relatives increasingly distrusted her, making it necessary for her to invest extra in defeating evil powers, making the Fogueira an even stronger conquest in which the amounts of money continued to increase.

Furthermore, following Bataille's "enigma of sacrifice" (1991), Fogueira sacrifices could be approached as expenditures that produce some form of sacredness. The intensity of believers' participation in successive Campaigns seems to resemble this idea of producing the sacred by becoming sanctified in an excessive ritual. The ladder to heaven that stood in the sanctuary during the Fogueira Campaign that I witnessed illustrates this idea. By doing something extreme, heaven is brought to earth. Outsiders condemn rituals like the Fogueira as manipulative, convinced as they are that believers only lose money in them and possibly destroy their lives as a result. Bataille, however, emphasizes that the act of destroying becomes a form of acquiring power. Where Bataille describes situations of rich people gaining status by showing their disregard for their excess, for example during so-called potlatches, Pentecostal believers acquire power by proving the strength of their faith when they sacrifice. This will however only be the case if they do it consciously—which is why Silmara failed.

Conclusion

In this chapter, I have reflected on the experiences of Pentecostal women in Maputo in relation to their failures and successes in organizing their relationships and economic life according to neo-Pentecostal ethics. The in-depth focus on a few active believers allowed me to demonstrate the effects of the incorporation of Pentecostal ideas and practices about responsible and intelligent faith that I encountered across socioeconomically upwardly mobile followers of Brazilian Pentecostalism. Their engagement with Brazilian Pentecostalism demonstrates that the Prosperity Gospel is not so much a reaction to the neoliberal environment in Maputo but is instead bound up with it and even reinforces some of its features.[20] Yet, this is not only the case in relation to a perception of neoliberalism and the Prosperity Gospel as empowering people, but also in terms of the ethical formation of the person who assumes responsibility for success or failure in life. Lying at the center is a religious ethical code that places the individual right in the middle of market forces that not only shape economic but also sociocultural life, including marriages and relationships. In contrast to prevalent ideas that churches help members that are vulnerable socially and economically (for a discussion, see Van Dijk 2010 and Van Wyk 2011), Brazilian Pentecostal pastors teach that every believer must "test God" by their actions of faith, risking bankruptcy and exclusion from social security networks, such as in the case of Silmara. In case of no "return on investment," pastors explain that the sacrifices and other actions of faith have not been done with determination and many converts do indeed blame their failure on their own inability to change their lives. How believers perceive their moral failure appears to be related to the generation they belong to or to the extent to which they have become acquainted with the challenges of a neoliberal society. Compared to the older generation, young Pentecostals seemed better equipped to deal with the demands placed on them. They had clearer goals and left the church sooner if they felt their lives were not improving. But these young believers generally remained attached to the Pentecostal ideology of self-responsibility and mostly moved to another Pentecostal church. In other words, the doctrine of individual responsibility has become so thoroughly ingrained among Pentecostal followers that when they "fail" they nearly always locate themselves in a discourse of personal responsibility.

Pentecostal upwardly mobile women in Maputo are displaying how their actions include being prepared to step out of well-trodden routines as a way to force change (see also Eriksen 2010). Crossing well-established sociocultural and moral boundaries is not being experienced as uprooting, and one's Pentecostal self-formation is becoming important precisely in the way one is able to destabilize socioculturally unified domains, such as lobolo or sharing wealth with kin. By partaking in Pentecostal practices, taking these calculated risks becomes a moral possibility that believers become increasingly aware of and learn about through trial and error. Pentecostal risk-taking is not necessarily produced by an external power such as the pastors, but rather a "calculated uncertainty" (Boholm 2003: 167) that agents can take or avoid.

Yet, believers can never be totally secure about the positive outcome of their behavior; even though they "give their best" they may be inadequate in their determination and temporarily fail in their faith, as in the cases of Elena and Silmara. They are acting in a spiritual war and are still prone to the Devil and can make mistakes. It is this tension that becomes inherent in one's Pentecostal ethical formation and is reinforced by the society in which one lives. In a setting where everyone is busy claiming cultural and economic space, as is the case in Maputo, Pentecostals come to experience how calculated risk-taking is a possible moral action enabling them to conquer *(conquistar)* these spaces with intelligent faith. In other words, in Maputo, the Pentecostal self-formation of taking calculated risks, which harbors the possibility of failure and success, becomes important precisely in the way that it becomes a sign of the believer's moral entitlement to prosperity in all domains of life.

Both failure and success in life are approached as the result of the effort of individuals who are more or less able to prove their competitiveness to God, who is believed to bless abundantly those believers who "know what they want." Even if it might seem easy to disqualify the image of a God who provides believers with enormous wealth,[21] the point is that the type of prosperity theology propagated and incorporated in Maputo, powerfully places a high level of personal moral responsibility on the believer to realize God's purpose for a prosperous life. In a time "where privilege has been divorced from wider social meaning and many obligations between members of different social groups have long since frayed" (Sumich 2016: 824), few citizens of Maputo believe that their government and other institutions (e.g., the extended family) will tackle issues like unemployment and wealth-sharing. The idea that they can help themselves by performing "strong" and "determined" faith seems to be the best self-governing technique to at least work toward improving their own lives, even if this enables the state and neo-Pentecostal churches to disengage further from their responsibilities to confront social ills (see also Bornstein 2003).

Acknowledgments

The research in Mozambique could take place thanks to a grant of the Netherlands Organisation for Scientific Research (NWO) and additional support by the VU University, Amsterdam and the African Studies Centre, Leiden. I gratefully acknowledge my Mozambican interlocutors, who shared their lives with me. I thank Daan Beekers, David Kloos, Mattijs van de Port and the anonymous reviewer for their helpful suggestions and insightful remarks.

Linda van de Kamp is trained as an anthropologist and based at the Department of Sociology, University of Amsterdam. She carries out interdisciplinary research on urban transformations, religion and ritual, and industrial and cultural heritage. Recent publications include *Violent Conversion: Brazilian Pentecostalism and Urban Women in Mozambique* (James Currey, 2016).

Notes

1. The Portuguese-Brazilian name of the church is Igreja Universal do Reino de Deus.
2. At the time, there were about eighty church branches in Maputo city—at least one in every neighborhood.
3. Genesis 28: 10–22.
4. The pastors explained that in the past people sacrificed animals, as they did not have money, but that today money is used. Also, unlike the animals, the money is not burned, but instead goes toward the church's expenses.
5. I use the term Pentecostalism as a shorthand for neo-Pentecostalism.
6. Central to this debate is the Weberian assumption that has been adopted in the academic study of Pentecostalism (Meyer 2007; Freeman 2012) and suggests that Protestantism has an elective affinity with capitalism.
7. See Beekers' chapter in this volume for a similar observation with respect to young Muslims and Christians in the Netherlands.
8. On the relationship between failure and responsibility, see also the contributions to this volume by De Koning, Kloos, and Robbins and Williams Green.
9. After a socialist era in Mozambique, the liberal reforms in the 1980s were meant to "reinvigorate the moribund nationalist project, to use capitalist methods to achieve the dream of 'modern prosperity'" (Sumich 2016: 824-5).
10. The names of my interlocutors have been anonymized throughout the text and their citations are my translations from Portuguese.
11. It should be noted that the religious classifications used in the Census as well as certain numbers are debatable (Morier-Génoud 2014).
12. http://www.uckg.org.za/growing-spiritually/faith-and-imagination/#more-20312, accessed 30 August 2014.
13. Costa (2007: 115–50) relates how desenrascar involves complex sociocultural and economic (kin) relations, including cooperation, negotiation, and manipulation.
14. The Pentecostal emphasis on taking initiative also attracts men, but women outnumber them.
15. Women have also become more selective in their choice of marriage partners, preferring wealthy partners (Groes-Green 2014: 240).
16. Elsewhere I presented the cases of Elena and Marta to discuss their changing position toward their elders (Van de Kamp 2012), and Elena's case in relation to "public counseling" (Van de Kamp 2013b). Here, I will principally focus on the consequences of their experiences for their faith.
17. The neo-Pentecostal Christian Evangelical Church Maná originated in Portugal.
18. While Pentecostal churches appear to mainly attract young people, I found that Pentecostalism is also attractive to older persons. For more on this, see Van de Kamp 2012.
19. I described Silmara's bankruptcy in another piece (van de Kamp 2010). Here I focus on the relation between her "failure" and her faith.
20. For a different interaction between the Prosperity Gospel and local socioeconomic structures, see Haynes 2012.

21. The Universal Church in particular has often been accused of running a money-making machine instead of a church (e.g., Mariano 2003: 51–55).

References

Anderson, Allan. 2013. *To the Ends of the Earth: Pentecostalism and the Transformation of World Christianity*. Oxford: Oxford University Press.

Attanasi, Katherine, and Amos Yong, eds. 2012. *Pentecostalism and Prosperity: The Socio-Economics of the Global Charismatic Movements*. New York: Palgrave Macmillan.

Bataille, Georges. 1991. *The Accursed Share: An Essay on General Economy: Vol. 1, Consumption*, trans. Robert Hurley. New York: Zone.

Berger, Peter L. 2009. "Faith and Development." *Society* 46(1): 69–75.

Bloemertz, Lena, Martin Doevenspeck, Elísio Macamo, and Detlef Müller-Mahn, eds. 2012. *Risk and Africa: Multi-disciplinary Empirical Approaches*. Münster: Lit Verlag.

Boholm, Åsa. 2003. "The Cultural Nature of Risk: Can There Be an Anthropology of Uncertainty?" *Ethnos* 68(2): 159–178.

Bornstein, Erica. 2003. *The Spirit of Development: Protestant NGOs, Morality and Economy in Zimbabwe*. London: Routledge.

Campos, Roberta Bivar C., and Eduardo Henrique Gusmão. 2008. "Celebração da fé: Rituais de exorcismo, esperança e confiança, na IURD." *Revista AntHropológicas* 19(1): 91–122.

Coleman, Simon. 2000. *The Globalisation of Charismatic Christianity: Spreading the Gospel of Prosperity*. Cambridge: Cambridge University Press.

Comaroff, Jean, and John Comaroff. 2000. "Privatizing the Millennium: New Protestant Ethics and the Spirits of Capitalism in Africa, and Elsewhere." *Afrika Spectrum* 35(3): 293–312.

Comaroff, Jean. 2009. "The Politics of Conviction: Faith on the Neo-liberal Frontier." *Social Analysis* 53(1): 17–38.

Costa, Ana Bénard. 2007. *O Preço da Sombra: Sobrevivência e Reprodução Social entre Famílias de Maputo*. Lisboa: Livros Horizonte.

Cruz e Silva, Teresa. 2003. "Mozambique." In *Les Nouveaux Conquérants de la Foi: L'Église Universelle du Royaume de Dieu (Brésil)*, ed. André Corten, Jean-Pierre Dozon, and Ari Pedro Oro, 109–117 Paris: Karthala.

De Witte, Marleen. 2011. "Touched by the Spirit: Converting the Senses in a Ghanaian Charismatic Church." *Ethnos* 76(4): 489–509.

Elmer, Simon. 2012. *The Colour of the Sacred: Georges Bataille and the Image of Sacrifice*. London: The Sorcerer's Apprentice.

Eriksen, Thomas Hylland. 2010. "Human Security and Social Anthropology." In *A World of Insecurity: Anthropological Perspectives on Human Security*, ed. Thomas Hylland Eriksen, Ellen Bal, and Oscar Salemink, 1–22. London and New York: Pluto Press.

Ferguson, James. 2013. "Declarations of Dependence: Labour, Personhood, and Welfare in Southern Africa." *Journal of the Royal Anthropological Institute* 19(2): 223–242.

Frahm-Arp, Maria. 2010. *Professional Women in South African Pentecostal Charismatic Churches*. Leiden: Brill.

Freeman, Dena., ed. 2012. *Pentecostalism and Development: Churches, NGOs and Social Change in Africa*. Basingstoke: Palgrave Macmillan.

Freston, Paul. 2005. "The Universal Church of the Kingdom of God: A Brazilian Church Finds Success in Southern Africa." *Journal of Religion in Africa* 35(1): 33–65.

Gifford, Paul. 2004. *Ghana's New Christianity: Pentecostalism in a Globalising African Economy.* London: Hurst.

Groes-Green, Christian. 2014. "Journeys of Patronage: Moral Economies of Transactional Sex, Kinship, and Female Migration from Mozambique to Europe." *Journal of the Royal Anthropological Institute* 20(2): 237–255.

Haynes, Naomi. 2012. "Pentecostalism and the Morality of Money: Prosperity, Inequality, and Religious Sociality on the Zambian Copperbelt." *Journal of the Royal Anthropological Institute* 18: 123–139.

INE (Instituto Nacional de Estatística). 2010. *III Recenseamento Geral da População e Habitação 2007: Resultados Definitivos - Moçambique.* Maputo: Instituto Nacional de Estatística.

Lambek, Michael. 2000. "The Anthropology of Religion and the Quarrel between Poetry and Philosophy." *Current Anthropology* 41(3): 309–320.

Lima, Diana. 2007. "Trabalho, mudança de vida e prosperidade entre fiéis da Igreja Universaldo Reino de Deus." *Religião e Sociedade* 27(1): 132–55.

Luhmann, Niklas. 1993. *Risk: A Sociological Theory.* New York: De Gruyter.

Macedo, Edir. 2000. *Orixás, Caboclos & Guias: Deuses ou Demônios?* Rio de Janeiro: Editora Gráfica Universal.

Mahmood, Saba. 2005. *Politics of Piety: The Islamic Revival and the Feminist Subject.* Princeton, NJ: Princeton University Press.

Manuel, Sandra. 2011. "Maputo Has No Marriage Material: Sexual Relationships in the Politics of Social Affirmation and Emotional Stability in a Cosmopolitan African City." Ph.D. dissertation. School of Oriental and African Studies, University of London.

Mariano, Ricardo. 2003. "Brésil." In *Les Nouveaux Conquérants de la Foi: L'Église Universelle du Royaume de Dieu (Brésil),* ed. André Corten, Jean-Pierre Dozon, and Ari Pedro Oro, 45–55. Paris: Karthala.

Mariz, Cecilia Loreto. 2009. "Igrejas Pentecostais Brasileiras no Exterior." *Análise Social* XLIV (1): 161–187.

Martin, David. 2002. *Pentecostalism: The World their Parish.* Oxford: Blackwell.

Meyer, Birgit. 1998. "'Make a Complete Break with the Past': Memory and Postcolonial Modernity in Ghanaian Pentecostal Discourse." *Journal of Religion in Africa* 28(3): 316–349.

———. 2007. "Pentecostalism and Neo-liberal Capitalism: Faith, Prosperity and Vision in African Pentecostal-Charismatic Churches." *Journal for the Study of Religion* 20(2): 5–28.

Morier-Génoud, Eric. 2014. "Renouveau religieux et politique au Mozambique: Entre permanence, rupture et historicité." *Politique Africaine* (134): 155–177.

Newell, Sasha. 2007. "Pentecostal Witchcraft: Neoliberal Possession and Demonic Discourse in Ivoirian Pentecostal Churches." *Journal of Religion in Africa* 37(4): 461–490.

Penvenne, Jeanne Marie. 1997. "Seeking the Factory for Women: Mozambican Urbanization in the Late Colonial Era." *Journal of Urban History* 23(3): 342–379.

Pfeiffer, James, Kenneth Gimbel-Sherr, and Orvalho Joaquim Augusto. 2007. "The Holy Spirit in the Household: Pentecostalism, Gender, and Neoliberalism in Mozambique." *American Anthropologist* 109(4): 688–700.

Pitcher, Anne. 2002. *Transforming Mozambique: The Politics of Privatisation, 1975–2000.* Cambridge: Cambridge University Press.

Shamir, Ronen. 2008. "The Age of Responsibilization: On Market-Embedded Morality." *Economy and Society* 37(1): 1–19.

Sheldon, Kathleen E. 2002. *Pounders of Grain: A History of Women, Work, and Politics in Mozambique.* Portsmouth, NH: Heinemann.

Sumich, Jason. 2016. "The Uncertainty of Prosperity: Dependence and the Politics of Middle-Class Privilege in Maputo." *Ethnos* 81(5): 821–841.

Ukah, Asonzeh. 2005. "'Those who Trade with God Never Lose': The Economies of Pentecostal Activism in Nigeria." In *Christianity and Social Change in Africa: Essays in Honor of J.D.Y. Peel*, ed. Toyin Falola, 253–274. Durham, NC: Carolina Academic Press.

Van de Kamp, Linda. 2010. "Burying Life: Pentecostal Religion and Development in Urban Mozambique." In *Development and Politics from Below: Exploring Religious Spaces in the African State*, ed. Barbara Bompani and Maria Frahm-Arp, 152–168. Basingstoke: Palgrave MacMillan.

———. 2012. "Afro-Brazilian Pentecostal Re-Formations of Relationships across Two Generations of Mozambican Women." *Journal of Religion in Africa* 42(4): 433–452.

———. 2013a. "South-South Transnational Spaces of Conquest: Afro-Brazilian Pentecostalism, 'Feitiçaria' and the Reproductive Domain in Urban Mozambique." *Exchange* 42(4): 343–365.

———. 2013b. "Public Counselling: Brazilian Pentecostal Intimate Performances among Urban Women in Mozambique." *Culture, Health & Sexuality* 15(S4): S523–S536.

Van de Kamp, Linda, and Rijk van Dijk. 2010. "Pentecostals Moving South-South: Brazilian and Ghanaian Transnationalism in Southern Africa." In *Religion Crossing Boundaries: Transnational Dynamics in Africa and the New African Diasporic Religions*, ed. Afe Adogame and James Spickard, 123–142. Leiden: Brill.

Van Dijk, Rijk. 2010. "Social Catapulting and the Spirit of Entrepreneurialism: Migrants, Private Initiative, and the Pentecostal Ethic in Botswana." In *Traveling Spirits: Migrants, Markets and Mobilities*, ed. Gertrud Hüwelmeier and Kristine Krause, 101–117. London: Routledge.

———. 2012. "Pentecostalism and Post-Development: Exploring Religion as a Developmental Ideology in Ghanaian Migrant Communities." In *Pentecostalism and Development: Churches, NGOs and Social Change in Africa*, ed. Dena Freeman, 87–108. Basingstoke: Palgrave Macmillan.

Van Wyk, Ilana. 2011. "Believing Practically and Trusting Socially in Africa: The Contrary Case of the Universal Church of the Kingdom of God in Durban, South Africa." In *Christianity and Public Culture in Africa*, ed. Harry Englund, 189–203. Athens, OH: Ohio University Press.

Vigh, Henrik E. 2009. "Motion Squared: A Second Look at the Concept of Social Navigation." *Anthropological Theory* 9(4): 419–438.

Chapter 4

FITTING GOD IN
Secular Routines, Prayer, and Deceleration among Young
Dutch Muslims and Christians

Daan Beekers

"I'm not an exemplary Christian, unfortunately," Rachel said when we spoke about the place of worship in her daily life. Rachel was a 24-year-old psychology student I had come to know during my fieldwork among young Christians and Muslims in Rotterdam. She had grown up within an orthodox Protestant family and later joined an evangelical student association and a Reformed church. She told me she had recently discussed the issue of making time for worship practices in her peer Bible study "small group" *(kring)* within her student association:

> Everyone is simply struggling with this, as in: How do I give it space in my life from day to day? That's just really *so* difficult. Because you get up, you directly start doing your everyday stuff and, uhm, at night you drop into your bed tiredly. Yes, that's the reality of each day. And what we came up with in the small group was that it can be very helpful to already pray in the morning, before you start your day, and that you sort of put the day in the hands of God. And I did try that and it is indeed very relaxed to start your day like that. But, when I say that now, I think: oh yeah, that also sort of slips away again.

Notes for this chapter begin on page 87.

At all times and places, Christians—and adherents of other religions—have grappled with feelings of imperfection. Indeed, Rachel's self-diagnosis as "not an exemplary Christian" signals a familiar trope among Christian and other believers. What is striking in her account, however, is the particular problem she addressed of integrating religion into her day-to-day life. Her statement about her morning prayer routine "slipping away" denotes the way her religious practice seemed to be inadvertently pushed to the margins of her everyday life. This struggle to devote as much time and energy on one's religion as one wanted to was widely shared among the young Christians with whom I worked. It denotes the particular challenge they faced of making and finding time for practices of worship against the backdrop of the rhythms and routines that shaped their everyday lives.

Strikingly, these young Christians shared this quandary with the young Muslims I met during my fieldwork. Consider Ismael, also aged 24, a student in econometrics in Rotterdam who frequently attended Islamic classes and talks organized by mosques or Muslim student associations. When I met him for an interview he had recently performed the *umra*, the non-compulsory pilgrimage to Mecca and Medina. Reflecting on his experience of coming back to the Netherlands afterwards, he told me:

> Over there things go nicely, quite peacefully, you're only occupied with worship. ... And then you come here, you have to go to school again, everything goes fast again, and again you have no time, everything goes fast, you are tired. ... Yes, you are actually almost kept busy to put it that way. In that way [my faith] does ebb. At first when you come back you are still pretty much at it [practicing worship], but at a certain point, yeah, then, yeah, you actually sort of re-adapt.

What Ismael felt he "re-adapted" to were the rhythms of everyday life that Rachel also described, rhythms that were less shaped by religious routines than by the routines of school, university, work and the general quick pace of social life. Ismael's remark about his faith "ebbing" reflects a sense of an unintentional decrease of focus on one's religion that is similar to what Rachel expressed.

In this chapter, I examine these common struggles among my Christian and Muslim interlocutors with regard to integrating religion in their everyday lives. I take these similar experiences as an invitation to what Olivier Roy (2004: 26–27) described, already some time ago, as a "transversal approach" that looks at the potentially intersecting ways in which different religious groups respond to the challenges of modern society. Aiming to move beyond the dominant frames that keep Muslims and Christians apart within both public discourses and academic studies (Beekers 2014), I approach my Muslim and Christian interlocutors as groups of young Dutch people who are striving to pursue a religiously committed lifestyle within a shared sociohistorical context and who can be analyzed comparatively as such.

Notwithstanding Roy's earlier plea, qualitative comparative research on Muslims and Christians has remained remarkably scarce. This is particularly the case in the context of Europe, where academic work on Muslims and Christians has been strongly divided between the fields of migration studies and the sociology of religion respectively (Beekers 2014).[1] The development of a self-consciously distinct "anthropology of Islam" and "anthropology of Christianity" has, while enriching the study of religion, further moved the analytical lens away from comparative inquiries across Christianity and Islam (Meyer 2016).

A productive entry point to ethnographic comparison, I argue, is an inquiry into the ways in which the religious pursuits of both Muslims and Christians are shaped by the conditions of a shared sociohistorical context. Such an inquiry can build on recent studies in the anthropology of Islam, which have called renewed attention to the ways religious endeavors are affected by the contingencies of everyday lives in particular local contexts (see e.g., Osella and Soares 2010; Marsden and Retsikas 2013). These studies examine how "Islamic discourses and practices are entangled in larger social and cultural systems, their contradictions, and the experiences of individuals employing and embodying them" (Simon 2009: 259). Similar concerns have been expressed in the anthropology of Christianity (see e.g., Scott 2005; Cannell 2006; Chua 2012). These contributions entail—at least in part—a critical response to tendencies in anthropological studies of Islam and Christianity toward a "non-reductive" approach to religion in which the emphasis lies with the coherence and singularity of religious pursuits (see Kloos and Beekers, this volume).

In this chapter, I seek to contribute to these contextual approaches to religion in two ways. Firstly, I suggest that such approaches can be further developed by a comparative analysis that focuses on the intersections between different religious groups that coexist in the same sociohistorical space. Secondly, I build on the broader aim of this volume to rethink the analytical separation that emerges in much of the literature between the pursuit of religious coherence on the one hand and the fragmentation of everyday life on the other. I examine in what ways my interlocutors' struggles with making and finding time for worship can be seen as not just opposed to their religious pursuits but also informing or even reinvigorating these pursuits. Specifically, while I show that these struggles with "fitting God in" can be understood against the background of the acceleration of everyday life under conditions of fast capitalism, I also describe how today's accelerated culture gives practices of worship a renewed impulse and significance.

Prayer, Faith, and Closeness to God

This chapter is based on fieldwork among young Sunni Muslims and Protestant Christians in the Netherlands, particularly in Ede, Rotterdam and The Hague, conducted between September 2009 and November 2012. The research focused on Muslims of Moroccan descent (but also included Muslims with Turkish and other backgrounds) and Christians of Dutch descent, who can be described as observant believers in the sense that they treated their religion as a moral guideline in their personal lives and sought to consistently practice their religion in their day-to-day lives. My Muslim and Christian interlocutors generally continued to identify themselves with the mainstream orthodox religious milieus in which they had been raised, but they also oriented themselves to revivalist tendencies in contemporary Islam and Christianity, as embodied by Salafi and evangelical movements particularly (even if many of them also took a critical position with regard to these movements). These young, revivalist-oriented Muslims and Christians represent two of the most prominent groups that are giving shape to a renewed religious vitality in the Netherlands (Roeland et al. 2010), a society that has witnessed a sharply declined influence of institutionalized religion on social and public life in the last fifty years or so (Van Rooden 2010). The people with whom I worked were between 18 and 28 years old (all those quoted in this chapter were between 20 and 24 years old), most were highly educated and all had grown up in the Netherlands.

The autobiographical accounts of my Muslim and Christian interlocutors commonly pointed to experiences of personal religious revitalization at some point in their lives, usually in their late teens, engendering a self-conscious, active and reflexive religious commitment. They aspired to what they described as a strong personal "faith" (while both the Muslims and the Christians used the Dutch term *geloof*, the former also used the Arabic *iman*). For these young believers, having a strong faith meant giving their religion a central place in their everyday lives, leading their lives in proximity to God and committing themselves to religious worship (see also De Koning, this volume, for a discussion of "weak" versus "strong" *iman* among Dutch Salafis).

Prayer played a central role in this regard. My Christian interlocutors commonly set aside specific moments during the day for prayer, often in combination with Bible reading. While their prayers varied in terms of content, they generally followed common styles, utterances and bodily postures. In their prayers, the young Christians sought to petition, "listen" and express their gratitude to God. The young Muslims practiced the *salat*, the prescribed ritual prayer, which ought to be performed five times a day (within set time intervals) and in a state of ritual purity. The salat is a structured prayer with a fixed sequence of bodily postures and utterances, but it also leaves room for personal supplication or petitioning *(duʿa)*. Both my Muslim and Christian interlocutors regarded prayer as a personal moment of connecting to, or even communicating with, God. They performed their prayers either individually or in a group—with friends, housemates, partners, student groups, or families. For my Muslim interlocutors, the Friday prayer in the mosque (considered to be obligatory for men) was an important communal event, as were the prayers in the Sunday church service and those in the gatherings of student associations or youth clubs for my Christian interlocutors. These communal settings were also significant as recurrent moments in which the young Muslims and Christians were encouraged to give prayer a central place in their lives and were offered formats and techniques to do so.

My interlocutors felt that prayer affected the ways in which they navigated their everyday lives. If practiced systematically, prayers were understood to be constitutive of particular moral dispositions, experiences, and emotions (cf. Asad 1993: 65; Mahmood 2005). For example, some of my Christian interlocutors pointed out that performing prayer in the morning changed the way they experienced the day. They felt that it made them more "aware," and anchored within them a Christian ethics that motivated them to stay away from sinful behavior. My Muslim interlocutors said that praying regularly, ideally five times a day, helped them to remain focused on God and harness themselves against temptations. Some explained that the salat offered moments during the day in which they could pause and reflect on their behavior and ask for forgiveness for what they regarded as wrongful deeds. The young Muslims and Christians talked in quite similar terms about the ways in which prayer ultimately contributed to an everyday sense of closeness to God. It was, however, understood that this could only be realized by making prayers an integral and habitual part of their daily lives. Prayer "nourishes" faith, my Christian interlocutors used to say. More than the young Muslims, they talked about their bond with God in terms of a personal relationship that needed to be "sustained," just like any other relationship. Some of the Muslims and Christians noted that when they did not give enough attention to prayer, they experienced a sense of "emptiness," or of "something missing."

For both my Muslim and Christian interlocutors, performing prayer was also an expression of—and a means of cultivating—a sense of being fundamentally dependent on God. Through their regular prayers, experienced as moments of return to—and reconciliation with—God, they could put their worries into perspective and become aware that their lives were guided by a supreme Being. The notion of dependence on God was also informed by their view of themselves as necessarily imperfect beings: the young Christians treated prayers as pedagogic practices by which they learned to build up a personal relationship with Christ, which was understood as the only path to redemption and deliverance from their sinful nature. For the young Muslims, prayer was a crucial part of a learning process of obeying and submitting themselves to God—correcting and disciplining the (carnal) self *(nafs)*, so as to move it closer to God and to salvation. For both groups, then, performing prayer was part and parcel of ongoing moral and spiritual work on the self, aimed at becoming closer to God.

While anthropologists have carefully examined how Muslims and Christians cultivate prayer as a technique of moral and spiritual self-fashioning (see e.g., Henkel 2005; Mahmood 2005; Luhrmann 2012; Reinhardt 2017), less attention has been paid to those moments and contexts in which people fail to practice prayer in ways they deem to be consistent or adequate (but see Simon 2009; Jouili 2015; Kloos, this volume). In the next section, I show that my Muslim and Christian interlocutors struggled precisely with making prayers an integral and habitual part of their everyday lives.

Struggling to Make Time for Worship

The Muslims with whom I worked regarded it as each individual's own responsibility to meet the requirements of prayer. As Farida, a pedagogical consultant, told me, it is one's own responsibility to keep one's "five appointments with God" during the day. "We attach a lot of value to appointments at work, with friends, with other people," she said, "but there isn't anything better than keeping to these five appointments and also really taking time for them." Farida's words put the emphasis squarely on the temporal component of the Islamic prayer. Yet, it was exactly this, taking time for prayers, that my Muslim interlocutors found difficult to accomplish in their everyday lives. This struggle was expressed especially clearly by Naima, a student in law whom I met in the context of a Muslim student association in Rotterdam.

Naima had "started to practice," as it was commonly put by my Muslim interlocutors, when she was around sixteen, particularly by trying to consistently observe the daily prayers. Yet, at the time of our interview, when she was 24, she had come to find it difficult to fit the prayers into her busy schedule. Next to pursuing a Master's degree in law, Naima had a job with the city council in Rotterdam for 24 hours a week. There, she lacked both an adequate place and the time to perform the ablutions and prayer, given that she needed at least half an hour to "do the whole process correctly." Describing the work pace at her job, she noted: "you are really doing so many things, and also meetings, and people coming in asking things, phone calls and that kind of stuff. ... Sometimes I'm really very busy and then I also really have my sandwich behind my ... PC at work."

On her workdays, Naima would "catch up" all the prayers she missed after she got home (a practice that some of my interlocutors mockingly called the "marathon prayer"). This made her feel dissatisfied with herself, as she was not "really doing it as it ought to be done." Apart from not following the Islamic prescription to pray on time, she disliked having to catch up her prayers in the evening, because "after a whole day at work" she would feel tired and her concentration would have dropped, diminishing the emotional engagement she would feel during her prayers. She explained that she tried to strengthen her emotional experience of prayer by cultivating, in her words, "awareness" and "conviction", trying to realize "what I'm actually saying" (when reciting a *sura*, or chapter, from the Qur'an during prayer), "to whom I'm actually praying" and "why I'm actually praying."

For Naima, this was a long-term, cumulative process. The emotional experience to which she aspired during prayer was *ihsan*, which, she said, meant "perfection," the "finest" *(uitmuntende)* form of worship and being "really very close to God." [2] Conversely, Naima pointed out, the result of not consistently performing one's prayers on time was that "you also come to have that feeling [of being close to God] less and less. Thus, you miss that feeling, and to get that going again [*weer op te krikken*], yes, you then have to, that doesn't come easily. You really have to strengthen yourself in that." Sometimes she was afraid of losing that feeling altogether, "because of all the other things, activities here in the world, that *that* will finally dominate and push the practice of your religion, like, to the background."

It is notable that Naima presented the impediments to prayer due to her work almost as an inescapable reality. She did not seem to seriously consider the option of privileging the religiously prescribed prayers over her obligations at work. "You have to of course live here in this, this world," she said. "So you simply have to work, you have to participate in society." The value she attached to her work reflected her professional ambitions. Naima aspired to a job in a government institution and told me, in an email correspondence, that her main motivation to do this work was to "acquire experience in a municipal work environment." Thus, her work was a relevant asset to her CV that could help her forward in her career.

Many of my other Muslim interlocutors, often as highly educated and ambitious as Naima, similarly seemed to accept as a fact the restrictions on religious practice resulting from their jobs and studies, even if they were— like Naima—dissatisfied with having to miss prayers. Most of them, indeed, struggled with performing their prayers on time, because of their obligations of study and work, the absence of adequate facilities at their workplaces, and a general sense of hurriedness and lack of time. At home, many of my inter-locutors were especially struggling to observe *fajr*, the early morning prayer that takes place before sunrise. They often did not manage to get up in time, particularly when they had stayed up late; for example because they had been studying for exams. In the evenings they often felt tired after a whole day of work, study or other activities, which, they felt, decreased their concentration during prayers.[3]

More generally, several of my Muslim interlocutors pointed out that the rhythms and routines of everyday life in today's Dutch society were unfavorable to consistently practicing their prayers. Some drew a contrast with Muslim societies in this regard, occasionally with Mecca and Medina (as Ismael did in the statement quoted at the beginning of this chapter), but more often with Morocco or Turkey, the countries in which their parents were born and which they occasionally visited themselves. The rhythms of Islamic prayer are part of social life in these countries, especially because of the publicly audible *adhan*, the call to prayer, which many respond to. By contrast, in the Netherlands one had to, as Idris, a student in Islamic spiritual care in Amsterdam, put it, "keep track of the time" oneself (my interlocutors often used technological devices like adhan apps in this regard) and to "activate" oneself much more to go and pray.

The struggles of these young Muslims with performing their prayers on time, then, were strongly related to the routines and the structuring of time in their everyday lives. Some also noted that they ran up against restrictions and hostile attitudes when it came to performing their prayers within the public domain (cf. Fadil 2013: 740–41; Jouili 2015: 155–61). Others may experience embarrassment to do so—especially, perhaps, when it comes to performing the ablutions (cf. Jouili 2015: 159–60). Yet, the major constraint my interlocutors referred to in this regard was a "daily rhythm" of life that "had nothing to do with Islam"— as Hasan, a student in political science in Leiden, put it. This conflict between religious and secular rhythms was clearly pronounced for my Muslim interlocutors, due to the relatively strict daily program of the salat. Yet, we should not be too quick in framing conflicts like this as particular to Muslims in—and as opposed to—a secular Europe, as some academic work tends to do (on this point, see also Schielke 2010: 5–9). To move beyond conceptions of Islam "as a unique or exceptional object of analysis" (Marsden and Retsikas 2013: 12), I have followed a comparative approach that places Islam alongside Christianity in Europe. This makes it possible to see that my Muslim interlocutors' struggles with secular rhythms overlap in significant ways with those of the young Christians with whom I worked.

Like the young Muslims, my Christian interlocutors often expressed their dissatisfaction with the extent to which they managed to set aside moments for practices of worship during the day. This was commonly discussed as a problem of "being busy". Echoing Rachel's words about her worship practices "slipping away" in her day-to-day life, Robert, a student in economy and a member of an evangelical student association in Rotterdam, told me that he often "forgot about" his faith as a result of the routines of his everyday life. On an average day when he had to work and hurry up in the morning, it would happen that he would take a moment for prayer before having lunch, or even only before having dinner, and realize that he had not yet "thought about God at all" that day. He felt that the practice of his religion often moved to the background of his everyday life, due to the "busyness of the world, in the sense that everything simply keeps on moving." Johan, a member of the same student association, told me that he did not manage to keep up with the Bible reading schedule that had been set within his Bible study group. He said he often "simply forgot it," because "it's sort of not part of your rhythm."

Many of my Christian interlocutors told me about similar experiences, some speaking specifically about their struggles to "fit God" into their day-to-day schedules. Paul, a Christian student in medicine, said: "[serving God] does not come by itself, you really have to choose for it, otherwise you indeed have no time left in your agenda, or you rather go and watch a movie, or there are all kinds of other things that come first." Charlotte, who had just finished her studies in social work in the town of Ede, similarly noted that "you have to do an effort for" prayer and reading the Bible, which demanded "some discipline and personal will." Isabel, a business consultant who had converted to Christianity a couple of years before I met her, talked to me about "things that keep one away from God":

> I think that for me the most important now is, uhm, time. That sounds a bit, well, stupid, but because I make such a full planning, God simply slides off constantly—to put it that way [laughs]—in my schedule. ... Also with colleagues, spending one Friday night going out, or doing something else. Your week is full before you know it and, as I said, when you are also away twelve

hours [a day; because of work] and you sleep seven hours, well, see how much there's left. And you have to do your housekeeping and you have to eat.

When she did find "time for God," as she put it, Isabel felt that such time was often "lousy" (she used the English term), as she would already be tired because of everything she had done that day. The consequence of having too little (quality) time with God, Isabel said, was that God felt "further away." Many of my other Christian interlocutors similarly felt that the busyness of their everyday lives temporally constrained their religious practices, reduced the intensity of their religious engagement and drew them away from God. These experiences are strikingly similar to the ways in which my Muslim inter- locutors felt challenged by the busyness of their everyday lives.

A notable difference between my Muslim and Christian interlocutors, how- ever, was that the former had to relate themselves to the prescription to pray on set times during the day while the Christians did not. Hence, these young Muslims faced the particular problem of integrating the prayers in their daily occupations, more specifically at their workplaces or universities, and they were confronted with feelings of inadequacy when they missed prayers. Young Christians enjoyed more flexibility with regard to setting their own moments for prayer and religious contemplation. Yet, this also meant that they could rely less than the young Muslims on a prescribed temporal structure for daily worship practices. Possibly even more than the Muslims, my Christian inter- locutors had to rely on self-discipline when it came to "making time for God" and fitting practices of worship into their busy daily schedules. Arguably, the risk of falling into line with the prevalent secular rhythms of everyday life was even greater for them than for the Muslims.

Nonetheless, my Muslim and Christian interlocutors shared the sense that their lives were so "packed" with activities and events rapidly succeeding one another, that there was often little time left to practice their faith. Even more, they often felt that worship practices were unwittingly pushed to the margins of their everyday lives or, as Isabel put it, that God constantly "slid off." While they aspired to consistently perform prayer as a means of getting "closer to God," they found it hard to realize this in their busy everyday lives.

The Acceleration of Everyday Life

Feelings of falling short, sinfulness or imperfection are part and parcel of religious lives. They are prompted by individual concerns over one's salva- tion, often invoked by religious authorities and deliberately cultivated within religious contexts (see the contribution by Robbins and Williams Green, and that by De Koning, in this volume). Yet, such senses of failure are also shaped in substantial ways by particular social conditions. The struggles of my Muslim and Christian interlocutors with making time for prayer resulted from the combination of their strong religious ambitions and a social context in which religious practices tended to be constantly pushed to the background of their everyday lives. In their hurried and packed lives, falling short of their religious aspirations was a basic condition of their religious lives. For these young believers, experiences of failure were continuously recurring, rather than sporadic and singular moments of "moral breakdown" (Zigon 2007).

Two issues stand out in the accounts of felt busyness of both my Muslim and Christian interlocutors: the time and energy taken up by their studies and jobs, and the more general sense of hurriedness and a quick pace of everyday life. These experiences correspond to wider social patterns. Studies in the Netherlands have pointed to increasingly widespread feelings of hurriedness among the population (Cloïn 2013: 161), a quickened pace of work and social life (Breedveld and Van den Broek 2002), and a height-ened encroachment of work on everyday life, whereby work has become more and more characterized by flexibility, multitasking and round-the-clock availability (Haegens 2012). Similar patterns have been extensively described in the international sociological literature, particularly in studies set in the Western world. These studies point to a restructuring of time that is related to two key socioeconomic developments: first, the onset of a new phase in capitalism that has been described as post-Fordism, characterized by the acceleration and increased flexibility of modes of production, consumption, and accumulation (Harvey 1989; Sennett 1998; Bauman 2000) and, secondly, the rise of "information society" since the 1990s (Castells 2000; cf. Eriksen 2001; Agger 2004).

Flexible accumulation, the 24/7 economy and the "digital revolution" have instigated a quickening of the pace of everyday life in recent decades and an increased fragmentation of everyday life (Sennett 1998). As Thomas Hylland Eriksen has pointed out in this context, "more and more information, consump-tion, movement and activity is being pushed into the available time" (2001: 101). Such acceleration under conditions of "fast capitalism" (Agger 2004) is not restricted to the economic domain, but spills over into other domains of life. Thus, David Harvey (1989: 291) argues that "[e]verything, from novel writing and philosophizing to the experience of laboring or making a home, has to face the challenge of accelerating turnover time . . ." This accelerated culture has been strongly reinforced by the emergence of the Internet in the 1990s and the continuous introduction of new digital media and technologies since then (Coleman 2010). It has been suggested that this kind of accelerated culture affects young adults in particular, as the demands and activities of their everyday lives—in the context of their studies, emergent careers, strong involvement in consumer and popular cultures, and experienced use of new communication technologies—can "feel all-consuming" to them (Smith and Snell 2009: 77). In their study of religion among young adults in the United States, Christian Smith and Patricia Snell observe that these people "would have a hard time imagining—if they thought about it—squeezing the demands of a committed religious life into their hectic and unpredictable schedules" (ibid.).

As young people living in an urban environment, studying, working, consuming and extensively using (new) media, my Muslim and Christian interlocutors, too, found themselves in the midst of today's accelerated culture.[4] They were receptive to the continuous influences of modern media, entertainment, and consumer culture (indeed, television, email and social media were often mentioned as things that kept them "busy"). And as I already pointed out for the young Muslims, both groups seemed to take the primacy of academic and professional pursuits in their lives for granted, negotiating moments of prayer and religious contemplation around them. Even though many of them criticized the excessive materialism and undue focus on "making a career" that they regarded as characteristic of contemporary Western society, most also pursued the modern ideals of a good life measured by material prosperity and professional success (Hage 2003: 13). They worked hard to obtain good university degrees and to set off on promising careers. The social conditions of contemporary fast capitalist society posed such strong challenges to my interlocutors' religious pursuits precisely because these conditions also entailed a realm of practice and aspiration in which they were themselves strongly embedded.[5] These conditions marked their daily routines and rhythms, their feelings of hurriedness, and their concomitant struggles to "fit God in."

Worship as Deceleration

The young Muslims and Christians with whom I worked, however, were not merely positioned ambivalently between the conflicting aspirations of religion and capitalism. As David Kloos and I argue in the introduction to this volume, recent studies that focus on the everyday contingency of religious pursuits have tended to disregard the ways in which such contingency can be found to affect and reinvigorate attempts at reaching religious coherence. It is this kind of dialectics that I observed among my Muslim and Christian interlocutors. I came to see that, in similar ways for both groups, the conditions of acceleration did not only constrain their practices of worship, but also endowed these with a renewed significance.

When my Muslim interlocutors talked about prayer, they typically put a strong emphasis on the Dutch term *rust*, which carries such connotations as tranquility, quietness, rest, peace, or peace of mind. They generally noted that the salat allowed them to temporarily let go of their worries, forget about the concerns of—what they described as—"this life" or "this world," and to connect with God. Asked why they desired such peace of mind, they pointed to the stress, demands or "chaos" of their everyday lives, to work and to personal problems. Fouad, a student in Islamic theology from Rotterdam, told me that his prayers gave him repose from the "hectic" character of his daily life and from his "busy agenda." During prayer, he said, "it's God's turn," you "close yourself off." Idris, whom I introduced above, noted with respect to prayer:

> You know that, that in any circumstance, however bad things are going, whatever stress you're experiencing, whatever deadline you need to meet, Allah sees

you, Allah knows that you're in that situation. ... So you know that you, that Allah is continuously with you. And prayer confirms that all the time. And that's a, yes, comforting thought.

Fatima, a psychology student in Rotterdam, told me that she would sometimes actually "spend more time" on her prayers when she was very busy with school, as this would give her a feeling of peace *(rust)*, and she hoped she would also be rewarded for it in her studies.

The embodied practice of the ablutions preceding prayer and the physical movements during prayer may be seen as both expressing and enabling the acts of letting go of "worldly" concerns and finding tranquility through worshipping God. Ahmet, a nineteen-year-old student in public administration who volunteered for a Turkish-Islamic association in Rotterdam, remarked:

> Because when you do this, right [raises his hands up to his ears], you say 'Allah is great' and you start the prayer. This has a symbolic expression as in: I leave *everything* behind that happens here in the world. And then I enter into communication with God, [recites:] *Allahu Akbar.* Then everything is gone. ... Just like a soccer player who says, like, that he forgets everything when he is on the field, well, it's something like that that you should feel.

In relation to this, some of my Muslim interlocutors described prayer as an extraordinary moment, temporarily taking them beyond the here and now. Mustafa, a student in law who had come to the Netherlands as a refugee from Azerbaijan at the age of twelve, said: "It's a feeling that you can only describe when you, uhm, do it yourself. ... We are now in a time and space, but prayer takes you above these, above time and above space. Really a, yes, traveling toward God."

The young Christians I met also regularly talked about prayer and other worship practices as activities that brought them peace, tranquility, or quietness. They also used the Dutch term "rust" in this regard, but did not emphasize it as strongly as the Muslims did. Many of my Christian interlocutors described prayer and reading the Bible as providing moments of tranquility *(rustmomenten)* in their otherwise busy and chaotic everyday lives. An important concept for these young Christians in this regard was "quiet time" *(stille tijd)*, a term they—like many other Christians (see e.g., McGrath 1996)—generally used to describe the moments of prayer, Bible-reading and contemplation that they set aside during the day, typically in the mornings and/or evenings, and that were directed at cultivating personal intimacy with God (cf. Luhrmann 2012). Quiet time entailed moments in which one became literally quiet, by sitting still and retreating from the buzz of everyday life. For my Christian interlocutors this often meant retreating to a private space, like one's bedroom, and "closing oneself off" from external, distractive influences as much as possible. Thus, Adam, a student in pastoral theology in Ede, told me that he deliberately created such moments a couple of times a week, switching off his computer and television and making everything "quiet" *(rustig)*:

Sometimes I also simply switch off the light in my room, then I only see the light entering from outside. Simply uhm praying in a delightfully peaceful [*rustige*] way and reflecting [*stilstaan*, lit. 'standing still'] about what is important in life, instead of going along with all that busyness and being confronted with your limits one day [*jezelf op een dag tegenkomen*].

My Christian interlocutors commonly pointed out that taking such a moment for prayer and reading the Bible in the morning—a moment of "focusing my thoughts on God," as Robert put it—brought them peace during the day. Similarly to Fatima, some of them noted that such practices of worship were particularly important in busy times. Charlotte, the student from Ede to whom I referred above, said: "I notice that especially when I'm very busy, I should actually take time for it [prayer and Bible-reading], because it makes me more peaceful [*rustiger*] and you can get the bigger picture again, so that you can continue again." In relation to this, prayer and reading the Bible were understood to help one to put things into perspective. Thus, Rachel, introduced at the beginning of this chapter, noted that these practices allowed her to "activate" feelings of peace and trust, which put all of her "daily worries," about her exams or her internship, for example, into "a bigger picture"—the "perspective of eternity"—that made such worries seem irrelevant.

These young Christians also found repose from their hurried lives by observing a "day of rest" on Sundays. They commonly sought to spend their Sundays differently from other days, by going to church, reading the Bible or other "edifying" *(opbouwende)* literature, and refraining as much as possible from work, study and shopping. Some, like Charlotte, also kept their televisions and computers switched off on Sundays, because these, she said, "can also very much hurry [*opjagen*] you." She told me that she experienced the Sunday differently from other days, particularly because of its "slower pace" *(trager tempo)*.

Strikingly, then, both my Muslim and Christian interlocutors emphasized the ways in which prayer and other practices of worship provided them with tranquility, rest, or peace. That is, worship offered them precisely that experience they missed in their everyday lives in today's accelerated, fast-paced culture. It has been proposed in the literature that religion can provide an alternative to, or means to cope with, the speeded-up culture of contemporary capitalism (Van Harskamp 2008: 16–17; Gauthier, Martikainen, and Woodhead 2011: 295). Building on that suggestion, I argue that for the young Muslims and Christians with whom I worked, worship gained a renewed significance in the context of today's fast capitalist culture. Apart from constituting an expression of their devotion to God and of their adherence to religious prescriptions or conventions, worship was felt to provide repose from—and indeed a slowing down of—the quick pace of life. Worship did not only require making time, but also entailed creating and allowing for a particular quality of time, characterized by deceleration and contemplation, inner peace, and, in Mustafa's words, a "traveling toward God." It was experienced as a time-out from the continuous flow of events, influences and incentives in everyday life. What gave this a tragic touch, of course, was that the very "busyness" that made these young believers long for worship, also made it difficult for them to integrate worship into their daily lives.

Conclusion

The young Muslims and Christians with whom I worked aspired to a strong personal faith, which to them required giving religion a central place in their everyday lives and committing themselves to prayer and other practices of worship. Yet, today's fast-paced culture, combined with the lack of generally shared religious rhythms in contemporary Dutch society, made it practically difficult to "fit God" into their daily schedules. For them, leading busy, hurried and accelerated lives seemed to be an inevitable condition of modern life. At the same time, the busyness they experienced also resulted from the kind of lives they themselves chose to lead, particularly when it came to the primacy they gave to their work and studies. Indeed, alongside their aspirations to religious commitment, they pursued aspirations to professional success, well-being, and the fulfillment of one's potential through one's career. That is, they gave shape to both a religious and a capitalist (work) ethic. In this sense, my interlocutors' lives were characterized by a moral ambivalence (cf. Schielke 2015) that manifested itself in their everyday lives through conflicting rhythms, routines and structures of time.

Yet, there is more to the relation between these—religious and capitalist— aspirations and rhythms than ambivalent coexistence. Accelerated culture also stimulated my Muslim and Christian interlocutors to invest in prayer and other forms of worship, which gained a renewed value for them as practices providing tranquility, peace and stillness in the context of their busy everyday lives. Thus, the social conditions of fast capitalism did not only constrain but also gave a new impetus to their religious engagement. Religious and capitalist aspirations and rhythms were not merely opposed, but rather dialectically related and productive of a particular kind of religious engagement in which the tranquility offered by worship was emphasized. This dynamic played out in similar ways for the young Muslims and Christians, who faced the common challenge of putting their ambitions of religious commitment to practice in a fast capitalist context.

I would like to end with a brief reflection on my interlocutors' approach to worship in terms of tranquility. To an extent, the value given to worship as a means of deceleration could be interpreted as a kind of secularization of religious practice. These young believers' search for tranquility through prayer resonates with desires for "slowing down life" (or what is called *onthaasten* in Dutch) that are more widely shared in society, particularly among the (upper) middle classes—captured by such concepts as "slow food" (Petrini 2003) and "slow tourism" (Fullagar, Markwell, and Wilson 2012). In this regard, the role that prayer played for them seems to resemble the role that yoga, mindfulness exercises or wellness retreats play for others. Moreover, if interpreted skeptically, their worship practices could be seen to provide only snippets of release from the quick pace of life, while these practices are subsumed in the fast capitalist economy as yet another activity that needs to be "squeezed in." In this reading, religion becomes incorporated in a temporality of "accelerating turnover time" (Harvey 1989: 291).

While I do see striking parallels between these young believers' approach to worship as a means of deceleration and other techniques of slowing down time, I would argue that my interlocutors' practices of worship also entailed a religious ethics that went beyond the conditions of fast capitalism. As I pointed out, for both the Muslims and the Christians, prayer played a crucial role in the ways they cultivated a sense of closeness to—and dependence on—God. It provided an occasion to repent for their felt wrongdoings and ask for guidance in leading a good life. Moreover, as Mustafa's notion of "traveling toward God" suggests, prayer for these young Muslims—as well as Christians—involved attempts at moving beyond the very organization of space and time that dominate their everyday lives in today's capitalist society.

Yet, it was understood that these ethical and spiritual effects could only be realized if prayer became an integral and habitual part of everyday life. It was here that my interlocutors often found themselves falling short. Time and again, the practice of worship appeared to be "slipping away" in their day-to-day lives. This made them aware that their religious endeavors were perpetually incomplete projects that required ongoing work and investment. Their practices of worship were part and parcel of such ongoing—forever imperfect—moral and spiritual work on the self, aimed at becoming closer to God. In that way, prayers themselves constituted attempts at coming to terms with self-perceived imperfections and inadequacies, without ever fully solving them.

Acknowledgments

I thank Markus Balkenhol, Margaretha van Es, David Kloos, Birgit Meyer, Bruno Reinhardt, Pooyan Tamimi Arab, Victor Kal and an anonymous reviewer for their helpful comments on earlier versions of this chapter. I am also grateful to Anton van Harskamp and Paul Mepschen for their useful suggestions. Further, I extend my gratitude to the people who participated in my research for sharing their stories with me and for having me in their midst. The research on which this chapter is based was funded by the Netherlands Organisation for Scientific Research (NWO).

Daan Beekers is a social anthropologist currently affiliated with the Alwaleed Centre for the Study of Islam in the Contemporary World, University of Edinburgh. His first monograph, an ethnographic study of religious commitment among young Muslims and Christians in the Netherlands, is forthcoming with Bloomsbury.

Notes

1. Most of the few existing qualitative comparative studies on Muslims and Christians in Europe are less concerned with contextualized comparison as such than with a cross-religious investigation into particular theoretical concerns, such as female religious agency (e.g., Bracke 2004). A recent ethnography that is explicitly comparative is Daniel DeHanas' (2016) study of civic engagement among young Muslims of Bangladeshi descent and young Christians of Jamaican descent in London. Other studies are co-authored publications in which scholars working on either Christians or Muslims have paired their observations (e.g., Roeland et al. 2010). In the context of Africa, anthropologists have begun to advocate approaches that "locate Muslims and Christians within a common analytical frame" (Soares 2006, 13; cf. Janson and Meyer 2016; Peel 2016).
2. In Islamic doctrine, ihsan denotes perfection in faith and particularly "worship[ping] Allah as if you are seeing Him … ." See Sahih Muslim, "The Book of Faith." Accessed 12 July 2016 from http://sunnah.com/muslim/1
3. Jeanette Jouili (2015: 58–64) has similarly described the struggles with implementing prayer in everyday life among Muslim women in France and Germany.
4. In her contribution to this volume, Linda van de Kamp makes a comparable point with regard to her Pentecostal interlocutors in Mozambique. She writes: "They are not looking for a safe shelter from which to judge the influences of the market economy; they are part of it" (p. 55).
5. While constructing a different kind of argument, Samuli Schielke (2015, ch. 5) has similarly pointed out that the Egyptians with whom he worked pursued both religious and capitalist aspirations. He contends that revivalist Islam and consumer-oriented capitalism share a strong sense of "perpetually underfulfilled aspiration" (ibid.: 125).

References

Agger, Ben. 2004. *Speeding Up Fast Capitalism: Internet Culture, Work, Families, Food, Bodies*. Boulder: Paradigm.

Asad, Talal. 1993. *Genealogies of Religion: Discipline and Reasons of Power in Christianity and Islam*. Baltimore, MD: Johns Hopkins University Press.

Bauman, Zygmunt. 2000. *Liquid Modernity*. Cambridge and Malden, MA: Polity Press.

Beekers, Daan. 2014. "Pedagogies of Piety: Comparing Young Observant Muslims and Christians in the Netherlands." *Culture and Religion* 15(1): 72–99.

Bracke, Sarah. 2004. "Women Resisting Secularisation in an Age of Globalisation: Four Case-Studies within a European Context." Ph.D. dissertation. Utrecht University.

Breedveld, Koen, and Andries Van den Broek. 2002. *De veeleisende samenleving: Psychische vermoeidheid in een veranderende sociaal-culturele context*. Den Haag: Sociaal en Cultureel Planbureau.

Cannell, Fenella., ed. 2006. *The Anthropology of Christianity*. Durham, NC: Duke University Press.

Castells, Manuel. 2000. *The Rise of the Network Society*, 2nd ed. Oxford and Malden, MA: Blackwell.

Chua, Liana. 2012. *The Christianity of Culture: Conversion, Ethnic Citizenship, and the Matter of Religion in Malaysian Borneo*. Basingstoke: Palgrave Macmillan.

Cloïn, Mariëlle., ed. 2013. *Met het oog op de tijd: een blik op de tijdsbesteding van Nederlanders*. Den Haag: Sociaal en Cultureel Planbureau.

Coleman, E. Gabriella. 2010. "Ethnographic Approaches to Digital Media." *Annual Review of Anthropology* 39(1): 487–505.

DeHanas, Daniel Nilsson. 2016. *London Youth, Religion, and Politics: Engagement and Activism from Brixton to Brick Lane*. Oxford: Oxford University Press.

Eriksen, Thomas Hylland. 2001. *Tyranny of the Moment: Fast and Slow Time in the Information Age*. London and Sterling, VA: Pluto Press.

Fadil, Nadia. 2013. "Performing the Salat [Islamic Prayers] at Work: Secular and Pious Muslims Negotiating the Contours of the Public in Belgium." *Ethnicities* 13(6): 729–50.

Fullagar, Simone, Kevin Markwell, and Erica Wilson, eds. 2012. *Slow Tourism: Experiences and Mobilities*. Bristol: Channel View.

Gauthier, François, Tuomas Martikainen, and Linda Woodhead. 2011. "Introduction: Religion et Société de Consommation/ Religion in Consumer Society." *Social Compass* 58(3): 291–301.

Haegens, Koen. 2012. *Neem de tijd: overleven in de to go-maatschappij*. Amsterdam: Ambo/Anthos.

Hage, Ghassan. 2003. *Against Paranoid Nationalism: Searching for Hope in a Shrinking Society*. Melbourne: Pluto Press Australia.

Harvey, David. 1989. *The Condition of Postmodernity: An Enquiry into the Origins of Cultural Change*. Oxford and Cambridge, MA: Basil Blackwell.

Henkel, Heiko. 2005. "'Between Belief and Unbelief Lies the Performance of Salāt': Meaning and Efficacy of a Muslim Ritual." *Journal of the Royal Anthropological Institute* 11(3): 487–507.

Janson, Marloes, and Birgit Meyer, eds. 2016. "Special issue: Studying Islam and Christianity in Africa: Moving Beyond a Bifurcated Field." *Africa* 86(4).

Jouili, Jeanette S. 2015. *Pious Practice and Secular Constraints: Women in the Islamic Revival in Europe*. Stanford, CA: Stanford University Press.

Luhrmann, Tanya M. 2012. *When God Talks Back: Understanding the American Evangelical Relationship with God*. New York and Toronto: Alfred A. Knopf.

Mahmood, Saba. 2005. *Politics of Piety: The Islamic Revival and the Feminist Subject*. Princeton, NJ and Oxford: Princeton University Press.

Marsden, Magnus, and Konstantinos Retsikas, eds. 2013. *Articulating Islam: Anthropological Approaches to Muslim Worlds*. Dordrecht: Springer.

McGrath, Alister. 1996. *Beyond the Quiet Time: Practical Evangelical Spirituality*. Grand Rapids, MI: Baker.

Meyer, Birgit. 2016. "Towards a Joint Framework for the Study of Christians and Muslims in Africa: Response to J.D.Y. Peel." *Africa* 86(4): 628–632.

Osella, Filippo, and Benjamin Soares, eds. 2010. *Islam, Politics, Anthropology*. Malden, MA: Wiley-Blackwell.

Peel, J. D. Y. 2016. *Christianity, Islam, and Orişa Religion: Three Traditions in Comparison and Interaction*. Oakland, CA: University of California Press.

Petrini, Carlo. 2003. *Slow Food: The Case for Taste*. New York and Chichester: Columbia University Press.

Reinhardt, Bruno. 2017. "Praying until Jesus Returns: Commitment and Prayerfulness among Charismatic Christians in Ghana." *Religion* 47(1): 51-72.

Roeland, Johan, Stef Aupers, Dick Houtman, Martijn De Koning, and Ineke Noomen. 2010. "The Quest for Religious Purity in New Age, Evangelicalism and Islam: Religious Renditions of Dutch Youth and the Luckmann Legacy." In *Annual Review of the Sociology of Religion, Volume 1: Youth and religion*, ed. G. Giordan, 289–306. Leiden: Brill.

Roy, Olivier. 2004. *Globalized Islam: The Search for a New Ummah*. London: Hurst.

Schielke, Samuli. 2010. "Second Thoughts about the Anthropology of Islam, or How to Make Sense of Grand Schemes in Everyday Life." *ZMO Working Papers* (2).

———. 2015. *Egypt in the Future Tense: Hope, Frustration, and Ambivalence Before and After 2011*. Bloomington and Indianapolis, IN: Indiana University Press.

Scott, Michael W. 2005. "'I Was Like Abraham': Notes on the Anthropology of Christianity from the Solomon Islands." *Ethnos* 70(1): 101–25.

Sennett, Richard. 1998. *The Corrosion of Character: The Personal Consequences of Work in the New Capitalism*. New York and London: Norton.

Simon, Gregory M. 2009. "The Soul Freed of Cares? Islamic Prayer, Subjectivity, and the Contradictions of Moral Selfhood in Minangkabau, Indonesia." *American Ethnologist* 36(2): 258–275.

Smith, Christian, and Patricia Snell. 2009. *Souls in Transition: The Religious and Spiritual Lives of Emerging Adults*. Oxford: Oxford University Press.

Soares, Benjamin. 2006. "Introduction: Muslim-Christian Encounters in Africa." In *Muslim-Christian Encounters in Africa*, ed. Benjamin Soares, 1–16. Leiden: Brill.

Van Harskamp, Anton. 2008. "Existential Insecurity and New Religiosity: An Essay on Some Religion-Making Characteristics of Modernity." *Social Compass* 55(1): 9–19.

Van Rooden, Peter. 2010. "The Strange Death of Dutch Christendom." In *Secularisation in the Christian World*, ed. Callum G. Brown and Michael Snape, 175–195. Farnham and Burlington VT: Ashgate.

Zigon, Jarrett. 2007. "Moral Breakdown and the Ethical Demand: A Theoretical Framework for an Anthropology of Moralities." *Anthropological Theory* 7(2): 131–150.

Chapter 5

THE ETHICS OF NOT-PRAYING
Religious Negligence, Life Phase, and Social Status in
Aceh, Indonesia

David Kloos

The first time I visited Jurong, a small village of some 500 inhabitants in the Indonesian province of Aceh, I stayed up late, chatting and joking with a group of male villagers. One of them was Dedi, 28 years old, and one of the more extravert figures in the company. A week later I visited again. This time I was taken in tow by Dedi, who showed me around the village, as well as the nearby market, rice fields, pepper, vegetable and coconut gardens, and adjacent communities. It was not until much later that I decided to make Jurong one of the main field sites for my research in Aceh. At this point, I was simply enjoying the opportunity to observe some of the daily routines in a place that was very different from the university campus in the provincial capital Banda Aceh, where, at the end of 2008, I was staying to set up my research.[1]

Dedi was born in Jurong. Orphaned at the age of twelve, he went to live in the *meunasah*, the village communal hall.[2] Relying in the beginning on his older sister for daily meals and other necessities, he soon learnt to take care of himself. He was unable to continue school and thus worked at the nearby market, loading and unloading goods from a warehouse owned by one of the wealthier traders in the area. As the years went by, Dedi increasingly ventured to wherever there was money to earn, although he always returned to Jurong, which he continued to consider his home. For most of the 1990s, he made a living by driving minibuses on the road from Banda Aceh to Medan, North Sumatra. This was not a job for the fainthearted. In this period, the armed conflict between the Indonesian military and the Acehnese separatist organization GAM (Gerakan Aceh Merdeka, Free Aceh Movement, established in 1976) escalated, turning large parts of the Acehnese North Coast into hotbeds of violence. The civil war came to a sudden standstill in December 2004, when a large earthquake and resulting Indian Ocean tsunami annihilated much of Aceh's West Coast and Banda Aceh, claiming an estimated 170,000 lives across the province. For Dedi, ironically, the disaster also had a positive effect. Hundreds of humanitarian organizations flocked to the region to provide emergency relief, and they were badly in need of skilled workers. For three years, he worked as a driver for different international organizations, allowing him to save money and to start thinking about the next stage of his life, beginning with the prospect of marriage.

One day, during those early visits to Jurong, Dedi and I headed to the meunasah to take a bath, after hours of touring the countryside. Dusk was setting in and the call to prayer had sounded. Some twenty to thirty men trickled into the meunasah for congregational prayer. I expected Dedi to join them, so I took a seat on a bamboo bench on the edge of the compound. Instead, he signaled me to follow him into one of the small wooden buildings erected on the side. This, it turned out, was Dedi's home. He closed the door and as the voices of the men penetrated the thin wooden walls we lit a cigarette and chatted. Dedi showed me a picture of a young woman. She was nineteen years old and she lived in Lhokseumawe, North Aceh, some six hours from Jurong. They planned to get married soon.

After a while, our conversation fell silent. Dedi turned on his TV and pulled out a pile of pirated DVDs from a cardboard box. We watched an episode of *Upin & Ipin*, an animated TV show from Malaysia—hugely popular in Indonesia—featuring a pair of twin toddlers learning basic Islamic lessons as they go about their daily adventures in a rural Malay village. Puzzled by this move to put on a religious program for children while his fellow villagers were praying right next to us, I asked Dedi what he liked about the show. He shrugged. "Nothing special. This is just basic stuff." He was silent for a while. Then he added: "I know these things. It is just a reminder [*peringatan*]." He got up. "Come on, let's have coffee."

The Ethics of Not-Praying

This chapter is based on ethnographic research in Aceh, carried out between 2008 and 2012 in two locations: Jurong and a tsunami-affected neighborhood in Banda Aceh. During this period, I frequently met Dedi. It became clear to me that, among his fellow villagers, he was known as someone who did not pray. As one of my regular interlocutors in Jurong—male, mid twenties, on good terms with Dedi—told me: "The whole village knows that Dedi doesn't pray. I think he knows how to. He just doesn't, or seldom." When I asked him whether he thought this was a problem, for Dedi or for his fellow villagers, he said: "In Islam, prayer is obligatory [*wajib*]. Actually, according to the [Islamic] law [*hukum*], the father of his fiancée [*wali*, lit. "guardian"] should not consent with the marriage. But the *imam* and the *geuchik* [village head] support him. I think they remind him to pray more often. And things can still change."

Aceh has been regarded for a long time as a particularly pious part of Indonesia. Expressions of and concerns about normative Islam have been particularly salient since the implementation, beginning in the early 2000s, of a local formulation of Islamic (shari'a) law, which includes formal bans of several moral "vices," such as gambling, the use of alcohol and other intoxicants, and sexual deviancy (adultery, illicit proximity between unrelated men and women, and homosexuality). The implementation of shari'a has been a subject of fierce contestation and the extent to which the state is both willing and able to enforce the laws is often overstated (see Feener 2013). Its impact has nonetheless been significant. Public conduct and expressions are increasingly judged, by state and societal actors, on the basis of a legalist and scripturalist interpretation of Islam. An important factor, in this regard, is the aftermath and memory of the 2004 tsunami, which led to a surge of public piety and a rather broadly shared view that the disaster constituted a warning from God that the Acehnese should live up to their name as pious Muslims (see Kloos 2015; Samuels 2015b).

According to most religious authorities in Aceh, as well as Dedi and his fellow villagers, neglect of the five prescribed daily prayers in Islam *(salat)* should not be taken lightheartedly. They saw it as a form of moral failure, because it stood in the way of becoming a good Muslim.[3] Yet, in the course of my fieldwork, it also became clear to me that Dedi's slackness in worship had only a limited effect on his social standing in Jurong, both among his fellow villagers and among prominent religious experts in the area. Taking this observation as a point of departure, this chapter poses the following deceptively simple question: How is it possible, in a place where Islam has such a prominent position in public debates about individual and collective morality, that an ostentatious failure to carry out one of the most basic ritual requirements is accepted so easily—casually even—not just by the general population but by religious leaders as well?

One way to approach this problem would be to emphasize how nonreligious forms of identification and mutual solidarity trump religion in everyday situations. Indeed, as I will show, Dedi's status as a "local" *(orang asli)* and the way in which he positioned himself, consciously, as part of the village community goes some way in explaining why his religious negligence did not result in more friction. It would be a mistake, however, to place the social acceptance of Dedi's behavior entirely outside the framework of lived religion. Everyday moral judgments in Jurong were based on a set of distinctly religious ideas about personal responsibility, integrity, and intention. This chapter shows that Dedi's religious negligence provoked a reflexive and ongoing engagement both with his own religiosity and with his place in the village community. It thus builds on the larger premise of this volume, namely that experiences of moral failure are often at the center of lived religion and ethical formation. I am particularly concerned with the relationship between religious commitment, perceptions of social and individual responsibility, and life phase. Both in the case of Dedi and in the case of many other young men and women I came to know during my stay in Aceh, the perception of religious shortcomings and its impact on individual religiosity was closely related to the transition from youth to adulthood. Put briefly, I argue that Dedi's negligence in prayer reflected an ethical mode that built on and incorporated, rather than excluded, senses of failure.

Most studies of salat (Islamic prayer) are concerned with its meanings or effects. They focus on what is achieved, cultivated or communicated through its performance (see, e.g., Bowen 1989; Parkin and Headley 2000; Mahmood 2001; Henkel 2005). Less attention is paid to the question of what happens when people fail to achieve, cultivate, or communicate, even if this goes against their own wish (cf. Beekers, this volume). Gregory Simon's (2009) discussion of the practice of salat in West Sumatra, Indonesia, is an exception. Simon notes that—in contrast to the emphasis placed by Saba Mahmood on the role of prayer in the pursuit of a state of ethical perfection—religious experiences in West Sumatra are often perceived as "incoherent" or "inconsistent," and, moreover, generally less rooted in an ideology of Islamic orthodoxy. He agrees with Mahmood, however, on the point that the salat, when "properly" performed, constitutes a site for the formation of "moral selves." When things go wrong—for example, when people think that they are not praying enough, when they feel they cannot fully concentrate or get the prayer "right," or when they stop praying altogether—it leaves people in states of "uncertainty" or "anxiety" (Simon 2009: 271). While this may certainly be the case for some (or many) Muslims, in West Sumatra or elsewhere, the case of Dedi suggests that there is also another side to these self-perceived shortcomings, one that is productive and creative, and that contributes to rather than damages individual processes of ethical formation.

There is much common ground between the present chapter and a chapter by Liza Debevec (2012) on explanations for not-praying and "postponing piety" in Burkina Faso. Debevec's interlocutors explained that their situations made it difficult or impossible for them to act as pious Muslims. She observes a "culturally accepted understanding" that "people can postpone the act of prayer and pious behavior to a time when this is deemed both necessary and appropriate and thus also easier" (Debevec 2012: 33). Debevec frames these explanations in anthropological theories about the complexity of everyday life and the various tactics and negotiations that this complexity requires. The "act of postponing prayer and pious behavior," she argues, is a "sign of individuals' struggle with the constraints of complex life under conditions of an economically harsh environment, which is not made any easier by the very strict and detailed prescriptions of a proper life as a Muslim" (Debevec 2012: 44). This chapter resonates with Debevec's argument insofar as it shows the importance of life stages when it comes to judging perceived religious shortcomings. The analysis in terms of negotiating "complex" lives, however, I find unsatisfying.

Instead of a "tactic" to navigate or negotiate the complexities of everyday life, this chapter approaches explanations for not-praying as an indication of a particular ethical mode—that is, of the ways in which negligence is thought to contribute to personal, lifelong and often unpredictable processes of ethical improvement.

As Daan Beekers and I explain in the introduction to this volume, our focus on moral failure is part of a broader trend in anthropology to study expressions of uncertainty, doubt and imperfection as grounds for action. Particularly relevant for the purpose of this chapter is Elizabeth Cooper and David Pratten's (2015) work on uncertainty and their emphasis on the "subjunctive subject." A "theory of uncertainty," they posit, is "best understood as a theory of action in the 'subjunctive mood'—action that attends to that yet to happen" (Cooper and Pratten 2015: 3, citing Wagner-Pacifici 2000). As Annemarie Samuels (2015a: 230–31) has shown in her work on child-trafficking rumors in post-tsunami Aceh, subjunctive narrative elements—the salience of "different possible realities" and the expressed need to retain "multiple perspectives and alternatives in an open-ended reality"—offer a crucial entry point for studying both the impact and the production of uncertainty in a society marked by great suffering and change. As I will show, dealings with everyday religious negligence in present-day Aceh are equally colored by subjunctive expressions. Life-stage transitions and the need to maintain or increase social status depend both on things achieved and a language of intention, producing moral flexibility both on the part of individual believers and on the part of their social environments.

A biographical approach enables me to analyze the "open-ended" nature of personal religiosity and the "contingencies of life trajectories" (Cooper and Pratten 2015: 13). It allows exploring the extent to which the possibility of divergent life trajectories is sanctioned in a place marked by social control and the rise of normative Islam. An individual case contains the necessary detail to analyze these contingencies. At the same time, the case of Dedi serves to demonstrate a more broadly shared religious ethics that was framed, for an important part, in subjunctive terms. Before exploring this in more detail, let me provide some more context and discuss the changing place of worship *(ibadah)* in Acehnese public discourse.

Worship, Discipline, and the Making of the Religious Subject in Aceh

In Aceh, like in many other places, salat is seen as the strongest and most direct form of communication between the individual believer and God (cf. Beekers, this volume). At the same time, congregational prayer, through its reference to ritual unity, is regarded as key to preserving the unity and integrity of the Muslim community as a whole (cf. Henkel 2005). What distinguishes salat from other basic religious duties (such as fasting or giving alms) is that, in everyday rhetoric, it is often given so much weight that it appears to stand for one's personal morality entirely. Thus, my host mother in Jurong, when criticizing the behavior of others (a market trader known to be a fraud, an unpopular politician, a villager making wrongful claims to public services), would sometimes conclude (and apparently make her point), simply by declaring that "he doesn't pray." My goal in this section is to discuss how statements about salat in Aceh are both rooted in and detached from successive attempts by the state and other public actors to shape ideas about (religious) community and to regulate the religious lives of the Acehnese.

The relationship between expressions of piety and ideas about the "self" is historically contingent. Around the turn of the twentieth century, existential reflection among Muslim scholars and intellectuals on the meaning of their faith and the place of Muslims in the world prompted the emergence—throughout the Muslim world—of a reformist movement. Islamic reformists saw the interpretation of revealed knowledge as a responsibility of individual Muslims. They also thought that the oppression of Muslims by non-Muslim imperialist powers was due, at least partly, to a failure to keep to God's commands. Framing the quest for individual salvation in terms of a broader attempt to change society for the better, they inspired a surge of political Islam as well as a wide range of twentieth century social and political movements that sought to perfect religious practices and dispositions.

It would be wrong, however, to conflate the reconfiguration of the self with politics and discipline. As Francis Robinson (2008: 273) has argued—with regard to South Asia and in the spirit of Charles Taylor—Islamic reformism was accompanied by an "inward turn," a process in which "the new type of reflective believer meditated increasingly on the self and the shortcomings of the self." The twentieth century saw a reinvigorated debate among Muslims about the relationship between the development of inner religiosities and outward piety. As Saba Mahmood (2005) has shown, present-day Islamic revivalists, building on the ideas of earlier Islamic reformists but ultimately going back to Aristotle, pose that bodily disciplining is necessary to cultivate ("inner") faith *(iman)* and thereby safeguard the future and the integrity of the Muslim community *(umma)*. As Reza Idria (2015) has shown, this idea plays a central role in the ideology of shari'a proponents in Aceh as well. However, as Anna Gade (2004: 48–51) has argued on the basis of her work on Qur'anic recitation in Indonesia, it is equally important to explore how inner states can be seen as a condition rather than an outcome of bodily discipline. "Inner," affective engagements with religious ritual, concerns and ideals can play a constitutive role in broader social and cultural change. This is both a social and a psychological process, bearing on the relationship between religious practice and knowledge and the construction of people's social positions and statuses (ibid.: 60).

Organized in the "All Aceh Organization of Islamic Scholars" (Persatuan Ulama-Ulama Seluruh Aceh, or PUSA, established in 1939), Islamic reformists played a central role in the Indonesian Revolution (1945–46) and the contentious and violent process of integrating Aceh in the Indonesian nation state. The religious discourse of PUSA centered on the practice of worship as a way to obey to the will of God and to strengthen, through the adherence to Islamic law, the bond between Muslims. Society, in short, was a "manifestation of *ibadah*" (Siegel 1969: 116). This was a very specific interpretation of the ritual of salat. "POESA leaders highlighted just those features of the *salāt* that supported their political project: the this-worldly discipline it imposed on the individual and the egalitarian and universal character of the congregation. They played down other possible interpretations of the ritual, such as its power to place the worshipper in a direct relation with God" (Bowen 1989: 602).

In the second half of the twentieth century, political Islam was domesticated by the Indonesian state. President Suharto's dictatorial regime adapted Islamic reformist persuasions to cultivate what Michael Feener calls the "*da'wa* paradigm," a synthesis of Islamic scripturalism, economic developmentalism and Indonesian nationalism that was disseminated throughout society by state institutions such as the State Islamic Universities and the Council of Religious Scholars. In 1999, one year after the fall of Suharto and as part of an attempt to end the protracted separatist conflict, the government granted the province of Aceh "special status," including a provision that allowed for the formal implementation of Islamic law. While this decision has often been explained as an attempt to discredit the (secular, ethnonationalist) GAM in the eyes of the Acehnese, the ideological basis of the current state Islamic legal system must be sought in the da'wa paradigm, which Feener interprets as a deliberate, systematic and long-term effort to reorder society on the basis of a coherent set of future-oriented ethical ideals.

Like the efforts of PUSA more than half a century ago, the implementation of shari'a reflects a political view that is directed, at least partly, at the realization of a "perfect" society. But in contrast to the language of PUSA, it contains few direct references to the practice of worship. This is not in itself surprising, for it would be impossible for the state to control the extent to, and manner in which, people carry out their individual prayers.[4] Yet, the extent to which the concept of ibadah is played down in government communication seems to go beyond the issue of mere practicability. As Feener explains, in the discourse of state shari'a, concepts of worship (ibadah) and belief (aqida) are accompanied—and to some extent overshadowed—by the (previously rather obscure) concept of *syiar Islam* (Islamic symbolism). He attaches great significance to the prominence of this term in public discourse, which he interprets as undergirding a "totalizing vision of Islam" (Feener 2013: 208–12). Discursively, it seems, syiar does more than categorize or regulate religious symbols. It serves to transform the environment in which Acehnese Muslims are taught and socialized, ranging from the use of the Islamic calendar to the architecture and design of public spaces.

The shift from ibadah to syiar does not mean that worship has completely disappeared from the vocabulary of the state. In an article on the danger of "deviant sects" *(aliran sesat)*, Alyasa Abubakar—one of the main architects of the state shari'a system in Aceh—focuses on the danger of praying "through [or via intercession by] other people" (such as religious teachers or spiritual guides) (Alyasa Abubakar 2013). Such statements reiterate a long-standing, state-centered discourse on the dangers of deviant teachings that goes back to the colonial period (see Kloos 2018). It is worthwhile, however, to consider Alyasa's words on prayer in more detail. "According to Islam," he writes, "the people who are most effective in their prayers are those who are most concentrated [*khusyuk*], sincere [*ikhlas*] and serious [*sungguh-sungguh*]. People who are not concentrated and not sincere, or [who pray only] for the show [*riya'*], even if they are very knowledgeable and have memorized many verses of the Qur'an will not achieve effect with their prayers" (Alyasa Abubakar 2013). Far removed from the earlier reformists' concern of creating (political) unity through ibadah, this statement nonetheless seems deeply reflective of what Francis Robinson termed the "inward turn."

This connection becomes more clear when I compare Alyasa Abubakar's statement to the words of Fendi, a 31-year-old inhabitant of Jurong, whose views about prayer were representative for the village as a whole. Prayer, Fendi explained, does two things. On the one hand, it keeps the devil at bay. On the other hand, it enables considerable rewards *(pahala)* to materialize, in this life but particularly in the afterlife. This will happen, however, only when prayers are sincere (ikhlas) (cf. Debevec 2012: 39; see also de Koning, this volume). According to Fendi, a prayer that is not sincere is the same as worship that is not taken seriously *(main-main dalam ibadah)*. The latter, he said, comes close to one of the greatest sins in Islam, apostasy *(murtad)*. The resemblance to Alyasa Abubakar's statement—particularly the suggestion that insincerity in worship may be worse than not to engage in worship at all—marks a domain of thinking about and reflecting on Islamic practices and their relationship to inner disposition in which the disciplining of bodies and the punishment of unwanted behavior plays only a subsidiary role. This is a domain in which negligence in prayer can be regarded as both undesirable and (spiritually) formative at the same time. I will illustrate this further by turning to the life of Dedi and the perceptions of his religious negligence.

Faith Uncultivated: Dedi's Not-Praying

About two months after my first visit to Jurong, I left Aceh. Nine months later I returned, this time for a full year of fieldwork. While I was away, Dedi had married Ika, the woman in the picture. He stayed with her family in Lhokseumawe at first, but when it proved too difficult for him to find work, he returned to Jurong. Back home, he started building a house on a plot of land, which he had inherited from his mother. At the time of my arrival, they lived in this partly finished house. They were expecting, and six months after my arrival Ika gave birth to a daughter. I mention these details to indicate that my fieldwork overlapped with Dedi's transition from a bachelor living in the meunasah to a married man and a father. This section starts with some notes of my private conversations with Dedi. I will proceed by giving several examples of the ways in which villagers of different backgrounds and different relationships with Dedi perceived and judged his not-praying. Placing these different perspectives next to each other, I analyze the connections between, on the one hand, Dedi's understanding of worship and his own religiosity, and, on the other hand, the complex of social relations that informed Dedi's attempt to maintain and improve his social status during the transition from youth to adulthood.

When I asked Dedi about the impact of his marriage, he responded that it felt strange not to live in the meunasah anymore. Although he played down the suggestion that his life had changed radically, he conceded that it had become more difficult to move around freely. "Ika's family is not here, so I cannot leave her alone for a long time, especially not at night." This meant that his options to earn money had decreased. For instance, he had to turn down relatively well-paid offers involving long-distance driving. At the same time, the period of *main-main* was over. Main-main literally means "play." In this context, it refers to a youthful attitude of approaching life with a certain lightness. The latter, for Dedi, included (among others) "bad" behavior—things that are "forbidden" by God. To put it briefly, there was a big contrast between his previous life of wandering and "misbehaving," of being in and out of the village, and of spending long stretches of time on the road, and his present life, which was characterized much more by fixed patterns and social control in and around the village.

Asked about the impact on daily worship, he responded with a platitude. "We Acehnese are Muslims. So we pray." Less of a platitude was Dedi's statement that he feared death and the punishments that might await him in the afterlife. He was convinced, moreover, that regular prayer might make his life easier. "It is as the religious teachers [*teungku-teungku*] say. Pray often, ask God for fortune [*rezeki*], and one will be rewarded quickly." Dedi tried, "bit by bit. I do have the intention [*niat*]." Yet, it was evident that, actually, not much had changed. Dedi found it difficult to put his mind to prayer. "Especially in the morning, I'm just lazy" (*malas*). Besides the challenge of getting up early, Dedi could not really explain *why* he found it difficult to pray. He said: "Perhaps, I am not capable yet" *(belum sanggup)*. Two elements are particularly relevant in this conversation. The first concerns the terms Dedi used, particularly "intention" and the suggestion of "(not) being capable yet." The second element is that, despite his fear of being punished in the afterlife, he seemed to maintain a relatively relaxed attitude toward his self-perceived negligence. Not yet capable, but with the intention to change, the failure to pray was a cause for concern, not a source of stress.

To understand this attitude, it is important to consider the fact that Dedi did not consider himself to be a "bad," or immoral, person. He made a point of his independence, his ability to take care of himself and his family, and the fact that he was a burden for no one. This perception of morality was connected to a sense of class-consciousness. As a poor person without property or resources worth mentioning, and without much family, there was no other option for him than to be honest *(jujur)*, at least most of the time, and responsible *(bertanggungjawab)*. The possibility of alienating his social environment simply carried too much risk. In case he would run out of work, or become sick, financial assistance by friends and fellow villagers would be vital. To this he added: "Those kids from wealthy families, they can just loiter. Not to speak of civil servants *(pejabat)*, they do not have to worry at all. I'm not jealous though. They have what they have. … It is difficult to find friends, but easy to make enemies. People can see that I take care of myself. But they also pity me [*sayang*]."

Dedi elaborated on the relationship between worship and social status by contrasting his intention to pray with the hypocrisy of those who, in his view, paraded their adherence to religious commands. Jamil, a young man who frequented religious study groups, prayed regularly in the meunasah and the mosque, and frequently donned "Muslim" wear *(baju Muslim)*, was nonetheless "lazy," "insincere," and "probably untrustworthy" according to Dedi. In his view, regular prayer did not automatically make someone "good." Here, one may recall the words by Alyasa Abubakar and Dedi's fellow villager Fendi about the ineffectiveness of prayers that are not "sincere" (ikhlas) or "for show" (riya). Dedi did not consider himself to be a good Muslim, but he did not consider Jamil to be a good Muslim either. Jamil's diligence in prayer seemed unimpressive to him, because it appeared to be motivated by an attempt to look religious in the eyes of others. At the same time, he presented his own moral faculties as, in principle, a productive basis for effective worship and personal change. Dedi, to use different words, was not without faith. His faith was, however, an uncultivated faith.

The idea that the transition from youth to adulthood implies a need to become "more serious" *(serius, sungguh-sunggu)* as a spouse, parent, and adult member of the community, as well as an individual believer reflecting on his or her relationship with God, is common in Aceh. It is often expressed in subjunctive terms, with an emphasis on intentions and the possibility of future change. Dedi's words resonate with those of young men in Ethiopia— Muslims and Christians—who, according to Marco Di Nunzio (2015: 161), "embrace uncertainty" to clutch the "chances" still to be found and the time that is still left to "change their lives." This attitude, he argues, often results in a deeper engagement with religious practices and the "cultivation of a good relationship with God" (Di Nunzio 2015:162). My argument is different in a subtle way. In the case of Di Nunzio's interlocutors, personal religious change was taking place in the present. In Dedi's case, religious transformation was placed, like other intentions, in an unspecified future. Let me continue by discussing how fellow villagers approached and looked at Dedi and how they interpreted and judged his conspicuous religious negligence.

As I explained in the first section, Dedi was one of the first people in Jurong who took an interest in me, a stranger with no ties to the village or its inhabitants. We were roughly the same age, and he was as curious about my life as I was about his. Although, compared to some of my other interlocutors, we never became very intimate, in my field notes about those early visits to Jurong there are some slightly worried entries about the possibility of being seen by other villagers as "close" with Dedi. As an anthropologist trying to get acquainted with my field, I was concerned about the risk of attracting (other) "eccentrics"—people on the margins of their own society—and of taking their views as representative for the whole community. These worries vanished early on in the second period of fieldwork. One day, I learnt that Dedi had been struck down by malaria. When I went to the local health clinic, it seemed that half the village had gathered there. The tiny building was full of people. In the middle was Dedi, lying in a bed, looking extremely weak and gaunt. The other villagers walked in and out. They came to offer mental support and to give alms *(sedekah)*. The amounts were small, 10,000 or 20,000 rupiah (U.S.$1–2), but given the expectation that Dedi would not be able to work for some time, it was indispensable. Dedi was awake, and he could speak, but he was too weak to take the money and put it away, so people put it in his lap, or they tucked it in his sarong or between the sheets, so eventually his body was covered with notes. This event, and the atmosphere in which it took place, made clear to me that, despite his conspicuous not-praying, there was nothing socially marginal about Dedi.

One day, while I was interviewing Nurmila, a woman in her mid sixties, Dedi stopped by. "Assalamualaikum," he said as he entered the house. He laughed when he saw us, sitting on the floor, the recording device between us. Dedi had just returned from Nurmila's family grave, which he attended to (pulling out weeds, restoring the fence, and so forth). Nurmila gave him a few more instructions and he left again. After an hour, he came back, this time in the company of his wife, Ika. She and Nurmila had not yet met. Nurmila told them to take a seat. In the meantime, my role switched from interviewer to observer and Nurmila's role switched from employer to mentor. She asked Ika how she was adapting and whether she planned to continue her studies (Nurmila used to be a teacher). When Ika told her that she had not finished secondary school, Nurmila sighed. "Well, that makes it difficult." After they had left, I asked Nurmila about her thoughts. She said: "It is too bad that she quit school. She is still very young. But Dedi is a good person. He can make a living. He has built a house. It is made of concrete!"

Nurmila's words are an example of the view of many older people, whose judgments of Dedi's not-praying were informed by the fact that he took his responsibilities vis a vis his family and fellow villagers seriously. Someone who was concerned more specifically with Dedi's responsibilities *toward God* was Abi, one of the leaders of a nearby Islamic boarding school. Abi occasionally hired Dedi as a driver and he was part of a group of male villagers who "accompanied" *(mengantar)* him to the village of his wife as part of their wedding ritual. He often reminded him of the need to worship. "When we meet," Abi said, I tell him that he must pray more often. I can do this, because he will accept it from me. Other people may find it difficult, although actually, it is also their duty to remind him." When I asked him whether Dedi should be worried, he answered: "Dedi is a responsible person. And he just got married. I am sure that he will pray more often, that he will go to the mosque." Asked whether Dedi's negligence should be seen as merely a personal matter, or whether it could also negatively affect the community, he answered ambiguously: "In fact, it is bad for the village. When other people notice, they may become negligent [*lalai*] as well. But in this village there are no problems.

Here, people pray. The real problem is when there is slander [*fitnah*]. Most important is that he knows, so I tell him. But he can only know when he is open for it [*terbuka*]."

Let me turn to Dedi's peers. Earlier, I cited a young man who, asked about Dedi's notable not-praying, emphasized that "things can still change." A similar comment came from Ridwan. He was from Jurong but had been away for a long time for study and work. Trying to make up his mind about the future, he divided his time between Banda Aceh and his family in Jurong. Ridwan described his student years as rather wild. Now he was preparing for his marriage and a job in a government office. One day, as Dedi and I sat and chatted in front of the meunasah, Ridwan passed by and joined us for a cigarette. We came to talk about religious education. Ridwan had gone through a largely secular education, except for the final years of secondary school, a period in which he attended a religious school in the afternoon. "In Aceh," he explained, "almost everyone engages in religious study for two or three years, sometimes longer." Then he grinned and pointed at Dedi. "Except for this guy!" And with a tone that revealed admiration as must as jest: "Dedi used to be the baddest boy [*anak yang paling nakal*]." Now he is married, and he will just become an ordinary person, you know, neat [*rapi*]."

As I have indicated, in fact, not much had happened in terms of Dedi's diligence in prayer. He was changing in the sense that he had got married, that his first child was on the way, and that his life was progressing, generally speaking, along the lines of increasing standards of social respectability. Judgment of his outward religiosity by other villagers was framed, for a large part, in terms of hopes and expectations. These views resonated strongly with Dedi's own emphasis on intention. In the meantime, no one questioned his faith. Talk about his religious negligence did not place him apart from the village, or the Muslim community (umma) more broadly. Instead, it reflected an understanding of ethical improvement as an ongoing and ideally progressive, but also deeply personal, unpredictable and socially embedded process.

Like Aceh more generally, Jurong is a place in which the transgression of social and religious norms can result in harsh, shameful and even violent corrections or punishments. Elsewhere, I have analyzed acts of vigilantism that were motivated by the perceived need to protect the good name of the village, typically against "newcomers" *(pendatang)* or other outsiders (Kloos 2014). The case of Dedi is different for two reasons. First, compared to other vices (especially those related to sexuality), a failure to pray is not typically seen as a threat to public morality. Dedi's not-praying was conspicuous (especially when he still lived in the meunasah) but it was not actively propagated. Second, the acceptance of his behavior was connected to the combination of his position as a "local" *(orang asli)*, a person from a strongly disadvantaged background (*anak yatim*, or "orphaned children" constitute a particularly salient category; cf. Samuels 2015a: 233), and a husband and father who—despite the lack, as yet, of religious discipline—demonstrated a resolve to work hard and to prove himself as a responsible member of the village community.

Religious Negligence and the Islamic Revival

As several anthropologists have observed, the stances of many Muslims toward the so-called Islamic "revival," and its normative and scripturalist leanings, are complex. Scripturalist interpretations and moral admonitions have clashed with long-standing moral, cultural, often place-specific values and value systems. Contestations have emerged around festive traditions, such as *maulid* (the celebration of the birthday of the Prophet Muhammed) (Schielke 2012) or other important ritual traditions (such as communal meals; Peletz 1997; Beatty 2009), Sufi-infused traditions of reflection, debate, and religious tolerance (Marsden 2005), as well as the local customs and social structures that govern the distribution of social status and prestige. Such frictions have appeared in rural areas, where "local" traditions are thought to be strongest, but increasingly attention has also been paid to ambivalent positions expressed in (sub) urban areas (see, e.g., Fischer 2008; Simon 2014). Ordinary Muslims, these studies suggest, seldom openly denounce or resist the normative pressures that have come with the Islamic revival, either because of the risk of being branded as "un-Islamic" or because they are convinced by, or feel attracted to, some of its claims, but not to all (see, e.g., Peletz 1997). For many Muslims, moral ideas and practices are characterized not by a simple or unambiguous choice between scripturalist piety and not so pious or immoral behavior but by tension and ambivalence (Hefner 2010; Schielke 2015).

While I am inspired by this literature, I am also critical of the way in which terms such as tension, contradiction, or moral ambivalence—and, at the level of the individual, the "unstable" nature of religious selves—have come to function, increasingly, as a kind of final statement when it comes to analyzing the nature of contemporary religion. An underlying problem is the tendency to reify expressions of Islamic scripturalism, activism, and political Islam, while in fact these expressions are part of a much broader and multifaceted historical development connected to what Francis Robinson (2008) termed the "inward turn." One of the important results of the inward turn, as I have come to observe it in Aceh, is a widely shared conviction to approach one's life as a personal project of ethical improvement (see Kloos 2018).[5] This conviction comes with particular pressures and impetuses—often connected to the expectations and responsibilities associated with particular life stages—but also, as demonstrated by the case of Dedi, with flexibility toward religious norms. This flexibility is not just a result of balancing different (religious and nonreligious) concerns (see Kloos and Beekers, this volume). It constitutes the very material of modern religiosities.

Dedi did not perceive his own religious negligence as diminishing or obstructing his faith. In a way that does seem to resonate with the central tenets of the Islamic revival, however, he perceived the need to consider his own flawed religiosity in the light of an ongoing, personalized and future-oriented process of ethical formation.[6] The important point to make, and returning to the central debate among Muslims about the relationship between outward expressions and inner religiosities, is that the values in which he grounded this ideal —honesty, sincerity, intention—were presented by him as a condition of rather than as a result of future change. It is tempting to interpret this stance as glossing over, or "explaining away" his weakness to overcome failure, but in my view it would be too cynical and unproductive to understand his motivations merely as such. Intriguingly, Dedi regarded his own failure to pray as sinful *(dosa)* indeed, but not, for that reason, unethical. I have chosen to take this interpretation seriously, and to consider his religiosity as a form of uncultivated faith. Actively cultivated, instead, was the recognition of "negligence" *(kelalaian)* and "incapability" *(belum sanggup)*, and the acknowledgment that, at some point in the future, he should become more diligent.

Like Nadia Fadil (2009)—who has written about "not-handshaking" and "not-fasting" among Muslim women in Belgium—I have approached Dedi's not-praying as a certain kind of conduct. The main difference is that the women interviewed by Fadil did not perceive their (non-)actions as a form of failure. For them, not to shake hands or not to fast was a matter of "human entitlement," reflecting their engagement with Belgium's "liberal-secular regime" (Fadil 2009: 451). Dedi regarded his habit of not-praying as negligence, not an entitlement. His situation reflects a more general stance regarding the relationship between moral failure and ethical improvement in Aceh. The temporal dimensions of this stance are quite different from the emphasis on urgency and immediate disciplining that characterizes many expressions of normative Islam today, including the ideology that lies at the basis of the state Islamic legal system in Aceh. The 2004 tsunami in particular strengthened the idea that immediate action is needed to keep Acehnese society from total moral collapse (Samuels 2015b). Attitudes toward moral failure, however, often do not share this emphasis on instant disciplining and urgency. Most Acehnese Muslims care about religious obligations. Religious negligence generally meets with disapproval. At the same time, the ways in which people deal with, and reflect on, their own religious shortcomings are often seen as conducive to the possibility of personal religious development. Placing the prospects for change in an unspecified moment in the future, the ethics of not-praying enables considerable flexibility toward personal processes of ethical formation, an aspect that has been under-recognized in the study of lived Islam.

Acknowledgments

The research on which this chapter is based was made possible by the Faculty of Arts (presently the Faculty of Humanities) of VU University Amsterdam and the Royal Netherlands Institute of Southeast Asian and Caribbean Studies (KITLV) in Leiden. I thank Daan Beekers, Annemarie Samuels and an anonymous reviewer for their generous and helpful comments on earlier versions. I am deeply grateful, finally, to all people in Aceh who shared their lives and experiences with me.

David Kloos is a senior researcher at the Royal Netherlands Institute of Southeast Asian and Caribbean Studies (KITLV) in Leiden, The Netherlands. He is the author of *Becoming Better Muslims: Religious Authority and Ethical Improvement in Aceh, Indonesia* (Princeton University Press).

Notes

1. "Jurong" and "Dedi" are pseudonyms. So are the names of all other interlocutors referred to in this chapter.
2. Traditionally, boys move out of their parental house upon puberty, after which they spend the nights in the meunasah, the village communal hall (see Siegel 1969). Although traditional Acehnese village life—including this aspect—has changed considerably over the past decades, when I first visited Jurong in 2008 there was still a small nucleus of five or six young men living in wooden shelters *(balai)* on the meunasah grounds, including Dedi.
3. "Moral failure" is my term, not my interlocutors'. As will be demonstrated in the sections to follow, my interlocutors used a variety of more specific terms and phrases to indicate perceptions of failure, each with—sometimes subtly—different connotations and implications for the personal, reflexive ethical mode analyzed in this chapter.
4. There is, however, an indirect way in which a focus on salat informs the practices of state religious institutions in Indonesia. Evidence of religious observance may be taken into account in court cases, marriage disputes, or (formal and informal) solving of domestic and communal conflicts.
5. Intriguingly, this seems to be a global phenomenon, as can be seen from the work of Daan Beekers (2015; this volume) and Martijn de Koning (this volume) on Muslims in The Netherlands.
6. On the relationship between intention, sincerity and ethical self-improvement, see also De Koning, this volume.

References

Alyasa Abubakar. 2013. "Aliran Sesat: Ciri-Ciri Untuk Dikenali." Retrieved 15 April 2015 from http://alyasaabubakar.com/2013/07/aliran-sesat-ciri-ciri-untuk-dikenali/
Aspinall, Edward. 2009. *Islam and Nation: Separatist Rebellion in Aceh, Indonesia.* Stanford, CA: Stanford University Press.
Beatty, Andrew. 2009. *A Shadow Falls: In the Heart of Java.* London: Faber & Faber.
Beekers, Daan. 2015. "Precarious Piety: Pursuits of Faith among Young Muslims and Christians in the Netherlands." Ph.D. dissertation. VU University Amsterdam.
Bowen, John R. 1989. "Salat in Indonesia: The Social Meanings of an Islamic Ritual." *Man* 24(4): 600–619.

Cooper, Elizabeth, and David Pratten. 2015. "Ethnographies of Uncertainty in Africa: An Introduction." In *Ethnographies of Uncertainty in Africa*, ed. Elizabeth Cooper and David Pratten, 1–16. Basingstoke: Palgrave Macmillan.

Debevec, Liza. 2012. "Postponing Piety: Everyday Islam in Urban Burkina Faso." In *Ordinary Lives and Grand Schemes: An Anthropology of Everyday Religion*, ed. Samuli Schielke and Liza Debevec, 33–47. Oxford and New York: Berghahn Books.

Di Nunzio, M. 2015. "Embracing Uncertainty: Young People on the Move in Addis Ababa's Inner City." In *Ethnographies of Uncertainty in Africa*, ed. Elizabeth Cooper and David Pratten, 149–172. Basingstoke: Palgrave Macmillan.

Fadil, Nadia. 2009. "Managing Affects and Sensibilities: The Case of Not-Handshaking and Not-Fasting." *Social Anthropology* 17(4): 439–454.

Feener, R. Michael. 2013. *Shari'a and Social Engineering: The Implementation of Islamic Law in Contemporary Aceh, Indonesia*. Oxford: Oxford University Press.

Feener, R. Michael, David Kloos, and Annemarie Samuels, eds. 2015. *Islam and the Limits of the State: Reconfigurations of Practice, Community and Authority in Contemporary Aceh*. Leiden: Brill.

Fischer, Johan. 2008. *Proper Islamic Consumption: Shopping among the Malays in Modern Malaysia*. Copenhagen: NIAS press.

Gade, Anna M. 2004. *Perfection Makes Practice: Learning, Emotion, and the Recited Qur'ān in Indonesia*. Honolulu, HI: University of Hawai'i Press.

Hefner, Robert W. 2010. "Religious Resurgence in Contemporary Asia: Southeast Asian Perspectives on Capitalism, the State, and the New Piety." *The Journal of Asian Studies* 69(4): 1031–1047.

Henkel, Heiko. 2005. "'Between Belief and Unbelief Lies the Performance of Salāt': Meaning and Efficacy of a Muslim Ritual." *Journal of the Royal Anthropological Institute* 11(3): 487–507.

Idria, Reza. 2015. "Muslim Punks and State Shari'a." In *Islam and the Limits of the State: Reconfigurations of Practice, Community and Authority in Contemporary Aceh*, ed. R. Michael Feener, David Kloos, and Annemarie Samuels, 166–184. Leiden: Brill.

Kloos, David. 2014. "In the Name of *Syariah*? Vigilante Violence, Territoriality, and Moral Authority in Aceh, Indonesia." *Indonesia* 98: 59–90.

———. 2015. "Sinning and Ethical Improvement in Contemporary Aceh." In *Islam and the Limits of the State: Reconfigurations of Practice, Community and Authority in Contemporary Aceh*, ed. R. Michael Feener, David Kloos, and Annemarie Samuels, 56–86. Leiden: Brill.

———. 2018. *Becoming Better Muslims: Religious Authority and Ethical Improvement in Aceh, Indonesia*. Princeton, NJ: Princeton University Press.

Mahmood, Saba. 2001. "Rehearsed Spontaneity and the Conventionality of Ritual: Disciplines of Ṣalat." *American Ethnologist* 28(4): 827–853.

———. 2005. *Politics of Piety: The Islamic Revival and the Feminist Subject*. Princeton, NJ: Princeton University Press.

Marsden, Magnus. 2005. *Living Islam: Muslim Religious Experience in Pakistan's North-West Frontier*. Cambridge: Cambridge University Press.

Parkin, David J., and Stephen C. Headley, eds. 2000. *Islamic Prayer across the Indian Ocean: Inside and Outside the Mosque*. Richmond: Curzon Press.

Peletz, Michael G. 1997. "'Ordinary Muslims' and Muslim Resurgents in Contemporary Malaysia: Notes on an Ambivalent Relationship." In *Islam in an Era of Nation-States: Politics and Religious Renewal in Muslim Southeast Asia*, ed. Robert W. Hefner and Patricia Horvatich, 231–273. Honolulu, HI: University of Hawai'i Press.

Robinson, Francis. 2008. "Islamic Reform and Modernities in South Asia." *Modern Asian Studies* 42(2–3): 259–281.

Samuels, Annemarie. 2015a. "Narratives of Uncertainty: The Affective Force of Child-Trafficking Rumors in Postdisaster Aceh, Indonesia." *American Anthropologist* 117(2): 229–241.

———. 2015b. "*Hikmah* and Narratives of Change: How Different Temporalities Shape the Present and the Future in Post-Tsunami Aceh." In *Islam and the Limits of the State: Reconfigurations of Practice, Community and Authority in Contemporary Aceh*, ed. R. Michael Feener, David Kloos, and Annemarie Samuels, 24–55. Leiden: Brill.

Schielke, Samuli. 2012. *The Perils of Joy: Contesting Mulid Festivals in Contemporary Egypt*. Syracuse, NY: Syracuse University Press.

———. 2015. *Egypt in the Future Tense: Hope, Frustration, and Ambivalence Before and After 2011*. Bloomington, IN: Indiana University Press.

Siegel, James T. 1969. *The Rope of God*. Berkeley, CA: University of California Press.

Simon, Gregory M. 2009. "The Soul Freed of Cares? Islamic Prayer, Subjectivity, and the Contradictions of Moral Selfhood in Minangkabau, Indonesia." *American Ethnologist* 36(2): 258–275.

———. 2014. *Caged in on the Outside: Moral Subjectivity, Selfhood, and Islam in Minangkabau, Indonesia*. Honolulu, HI: University of Hawai'i Press.

Verkaaik, Oskar. 2014. "The Art of Imperfection: Contemporary Synagogues in Germany and the Netherlands." *Journal of the Royal Anthropological Institute* 20(3): 486–504.

Wagner-Pacifici, Robin E. 2000. *Theorizing the Standoff: Contingency in Action*. Cambridge: Cambridge University Press.

Chapter 6

MORAL FAILURE, EVERYDAY RELIGION, AND ISLAMIC AUTHORIZATION

Thijl Sunier

Almost twenty-five years ago I witnessed a discussion in a Turkish mosque in the city of Rotterdam while doing fieldwork for my doctoral thesis.[1] The discussion was about a pressing issue emerging in those years. The chairman of the board of the Turkish mosque, a young man who was a socially very active inhabitant of the local neighborhood, proposed to organize a small event in the mosque around the *iftar* (the collective breaking of the fast) at the end of the holy month of Ramadan. He proposed to turn the ritual into a meeting to which the local community and a number of key players in the neighborhood would be invited. The mosque discussion provides an intriguing insight into the central theme of this volume and leads into the issue I want to dwell upon in this chapter.

The mosque was located in an area of the city that was in the middle of a thorough urban renewal process. For a successful accomplishment of the reconstruction process it was vital for the local municipality to include all residents into the procedures and to have an optimal communicative platform. For mosque associations it was a time of political opportunities and openings, but also of challenges and predicaments. Some local representatives of mosques considered the quickly changing circumstances as an important possibility

Notes for this chapter begin on page 120.

to improve their position in the neighborhood and also to negotiate a better location for the mosque. They would become important interlocutors for the municipality, and they could also improve relations with local authorities and neighborhood institutions. The 1980s were successful for mosque associations in terms of growth, but the relations with the rest of the local (predominantly non-Muslim) community were tense. There was minimal contact. The urban renewal process could turn this tide. But there was much more at stake. It was the time when a new generation of Muslims who had grown up in Europe became more and more visible in the Islamic landscape. They questioned the established associational status quo and the strong orientation of mosque associations toward the countries of origin. Many of these new activists considered a further rooting in the local community as more important than the maintenance of strong networks with the countries of origin (see Sunier 1996).

It was under these circumstances that some local mosque associations were thinking about the question of how to accomplish this. The aforementioned Turkish mosque was one of them. Until then, organized activities between mosque associations and the local population were confined to the regular mutual visits between mosques and churches, the so-called dialogue meetings. Most of these encounters consisted of the usual exchange of information about religious traditions and practices, drinking tea and expressing kind words about religious freedom and tolerance.

To invite non-Muslims to this very intimate ritual moment was a daring initiative. Today, these kinds of meetings are common practice in many mosques in Europe, but in those days it was a novelty.[2] As a regular visitor to the mosque for a number of years I had previously attended the ritual even though I am not a Muslim. Even for those who had doubts about allowing non-Muslims to these sacred Islamic occasions, my presence was acceptable as long as I would keep a low profile. However, the proposal of the chairman was of a different nature. He thought about opening up the ritual and to turn it into a public event; at least he intended to invite a limited number of people to attend the ritual and the subsequent meal at the mosque. The motive behind this initiative was to create more understanding about Muslim rituals and norms, but also to emphasize that the mosque and Muslims in general were an integral and cooperative part of the neighborhood. Some weeks before the discussion in the mosque took place he had raised the idea and shared it with some of his associates to learn what they thought of it. It was decided it would be discussed with the old members and the previous board.

During the discussion with the larger group of associates it turned out that some were vehemently against the idea. Others had serious doubts, not just about the practicalities of such an initiative and about the reactions of the regular visitors of the mosque, but also about the implications of the idea. Those who were against the idea of inviting non-Muslims to the ritual end of Ramadan argued that Ramadan is a renewed engagement with the ethical underpinnings of Islam. Introspection and ethical reflection emanating from the physical impositions of the food regime generate ethical sensibilities that tend to wane under ordinary everyday conditions. Some of the participants in the discussion referred to Ramadan as an ethical realm that by definition must remain exclusive and extraordinary. One of the participants stated that "we have to teach our children what the important aspects of Islam are. ... How can they appreciate that when we consider everything accessible for everyone? You take part in Ramadan when you want to become a good Muslim, not because it is an obligation."[3]

Those who initially came up with the plan admitted that it took considerable time, doubt, and ambiguity before they arrived at the conclusion that it was neither a breach with Islamic principles, nor a compromise with requirements of the non-Muslim environment as some opponents would argue. It was, in their words, an ethical choice completely in accordance with the "true meaning of Islam." At some point the discussion revolved around the question of timing. The transition from the end of Ramadan to the beginning of Eid-ul-fitr (or sugar feast, the Turkish popular name) constitutes a clear moment of passage. During Ramadan, Muslims go through a month of contemplation, introspection, and sometimes physical endurance. The beginning of Eid-ul-fitr marks the end of this period of effort and is an explicitly festive and joyful event. It is an occasion for inviting friends and family, to prepare an abundance of good food and to look forward to the coming year. To share this joy with people outside the Muslim community is a regular practice.

Now one might argue that the discussion in the mosque was not so much about ethical failure as about moral deliberation. After all, the discussion was about a proposed policy change that would intervene in a religious ritual. Yet a sense of failure was a crucial element of the process of moral deliberation that took place. In that respect the case perfectly demonstrates how these kinds of arrangements bear upon the wide array of individual ethical dilemmas and ambiguities that Muslims encounter on a daily basis. The fasting during Ramadan is indeed an "ethical moment." Following Michael Lambek (2010: 7), it is at the "... conjunction or movement between explicit local pronouncements and implicit local practices and circumstances." Although Ramadan is full of nondeliberative standard ritual practice, it also brings practitioners into a disposition where they step out of "... idealized reenactments of key scenarios ... ." Fasting is a form of ethical self-disciplining, a form of moral attunement (Hirschkind 2001: 624). The opponents of the initiative argued that when non-Muslims were allowed in it would seriously infringe upon these very crucial moments of religious experience, and, more importantly, it would lead to ethical neglect. It would inhibit proper performance and miss its intentions and goals and lead to failure. To turn this into a public event was seen as giving in to the pressure from the outside world. Why would they, as Muslims, let their rituals and sacred moments be intruded for the sake of harmonious relations within the wider society?

Those in favor of admitting non-Muslims argued that this was not at all against the rules of Islam or against the deeper meaning of fasting. Bridging the gap between Muslims and non-Muslims by including them in ritual activities was not a violation of religious norms. On the contrary, they argued. Sharing deeply felt convictions and practices with non-Muslims, or performing these practices amidst people who do not fast, reinforces the quality of fasting as a conscious virtuous act. In fact, some argued, isolating intimate religious practices from the outside world is an easy way to fulfill religious duties. It is not in accordance with the deeper meaning and it is actually not very sincere. But it was also a virtuous act because it would make Islam an inclusive religion. "This is precisely how the Prophet built the earliest religious community," one participant argued.[4]

The dispute was partly resolved by the decision to organize the public event around the breaking of the fast as it was intended, but a couple of days before the actual end of Ramadan. However, the debate was certainly not just about finding a practical solution for an organizational problem. These kinds of debates are moments of reflection about interpretations of rules and principles, about experience and subjectivity, and by consequence about the authentication of religious norms and principles, and of authority.

Everyday Moral Dilemmas

In the introduction to this volume, the editors, David Kloos and Daan Beekers, rightly take issue with the current overemphasis in the literature on acts of piety and religious perfection at the expense of insight into how ethical setbacks, ambiguous situations, personal senses of failures, and self-perceived lack of religious confidence, faith or belief are constitutive of religious self-improvement. They refer to a growing body of literature that addresses struggles, paradoxes, contradictions and ambivalences in the lives of individual religious practitioners, and they argue that failure and ambiguity are too often considered to pertain to that which occurs outside the boundaries of a distinctly religious realm of reasoning and acting. In fact, the editors state, self-perceived moral failure—that is, the feeling that practitioners have when, in their own view, they fail to act in accordance with religious rules, neglect religious duties, or deliberately do nonreligious things and think nonreligiously— cannot be simply disconnected from their religious ideals and aspirations. In short, moral failure is about "straying from the straight path" out of weakness, or for whatever reason and motive. Failure, in this sense, is certainly regarded by religious practitioners as a detrimental practice. Yet, what the editors put into question is the sharp dividing line found in the literature between virtuous (religious) acting on the one hand and "wrong," or "sinful" (nonreligious) acting on the other. Instead they propose an approach that includes moral failure as being formative rather than detrimental to virtuous behavior and ethical improvement. I largely agree with this line of argumentation, but we need a more subtle assessment of moral failure by clearly distinguishing between situations where it is reproductive and confirmative of religious authority and situations where it is constitutive of change and renewal.

An analysis of moral failure indeed provides insight into how, under what circumstances and in what particular settings success or failure comes about. Only when we gain such insight are we able to understand its efficacy from the perspective of the religious practitioner and its analytical rigor from a conceptual perspective. However, I would like to push the argument a bit further. A sense of failure occurs where there is choice and where practitioners make a wrong choice knowingly. Failure may be constitutive of moral self-improvement when an act is understood by the practitioner as wrong. Only then it becomes part of a personal narrative about morality. Failure then leads to self-reflection. One who fails knows that he or she does so; otherwise it will not be categorized as failure and hence does not work in attempts of ethical improvement. If we would include unintended or accidental acts that go against Islamic norms and values, or situations in which the actor does not even know that he or she is acting against rules, it would make no sense to call it failure. A classical case in this regard is the question whether unconsciously consuming something that is forbidden is a failure and thus *haram*. There is a considerable consensus among Muslim scholars that this is not the case.

I therefore argue that a sense of failure is by definition self-perceptive. It refers to what is considered the normative standard by the practitioner and how she or he reflects on that. It is the failure to act according to established Islamic principles that functions as the moral point of reference for the practitioner. What these normative principles imply is not at stake, so moral improvement then is also affirmative and reproductive. Under these circumstances we may define failure indeed straightforward as negligence of religious duties. Think of a Muslim eating during daytime in the month of Ramadan without legitimate reason. This can be perceived as a consequence of weakness, seduction, or temptation. If the "perpetrator" also arrives at this conclusion, it is reflective and may indeed become formative to virtuous behavior. I recall extensive talks I had with young Muslims who considered themselves "newborn Muslims." They lived a life full of sin, they told me, in which they did all that God forbade. After some time in which they went through a period of deep crisis, they found Islam again. Not very surprisingly they juxtaposed their lives prior to and after their rebirth in the strongest possible terms. Sin and negligence became a crucial element in their narrative because it made their return to Islam all the more explicit and outlined and made them able to understand the real meaning of Islam.

However, there are also situations in which rules and obligations are at stake, but where moral reflection leads to (re)authentication of religious authority, to reinterpretation, change, and innovation. As Jarett Zigon (2007) argues, as far as morality is applied as a conceptual tool by anthropologists, it has often been used much in the same way as culture: a tool that explains practices and convictions of individual actors by referring to an overarching shared culture. However, individual actors may not always perceive their actions and choices as moral interventions (ibid.: 132). He suggests that there are roughly speaking two approaches in anthropology to issues of morality and ethics in concrete situations and contexts. The first one rests on the assumption that morality or moral behavior can be recorded by observing deliberate choices individuals make in issues about right and wrong and to find out about the ethical references that legitimate these choices. The other approach is what he calls the dispositional/virtue approach. Virtuous acts are acts with the aim to train the body and mind to become virtuous. However, both these approaches, according to Zigon, start from the assumption that moral acting is deliberate acting and consciously making choices in situations of various natures. Both approaches thus start from the assumption that moral acting is a specific sub-field of acting in general. However, to consider morality and ethics as a specific subfield of human activity is to easily slip into the implicit argument that ethics is a matter of professionals and, as far as religion is concerned, of religious scholars and elites (Zigon 2007: 133).

What I propose here is to take into consideration what I would call the "total ethical scheme"—that is, to include everyday experiences of ordinary Muslims and concomitant frictions and dilemmas in the process of the (re) making of religious authority.[5] In the case of the mosque discussion about the iftar, the authoritative quality of certain Islamic obligations and norms was at stake, because the situation was not at all unambiguous and unequivocal, and there were no ready answers to the issue at stake. What exactly is perceived by practitioners as failure and why one does call an act (or non-act) wrong or sinful may not be clear/unequivocal/self-evident in such cases. Put differently, is there a consensus among religious practitioners about the criteria to judge these issues and from what point of reference? In many cases there is, but I am interested in those cases and situations where the ambiguity concerns the very definition of failure by religious practitioners, where friction and contention occurs, and where practitioners begin to reflect on the normative status quo.

During my fieldwork, a couple of years ago, I had a talk with a young man in a mosque in the Netherlands. He explained to me what activities they had organized with the mosque association and how they taught young partic-ipants what it means to live in a non-Islamic society. At a certain moment there was an indoor call to prayer. I asked him whether he should not go for the ritual prayer. He answered that the *salat* (Islamic prayer) is indeed an important religious duty, but "at this moment talking with you and explaining things about Islam is more important. It is also a religious duty that deserves attention and sometimes needs priority." Would he call his "neglect" of a cen-tral religious duty a failure? I would say no, he did not. Rather, he interpreted his conversation with me as a virtuous act. Not performing the salat at that particular moment was not a moment of weakness in his eyes. It was a deci-sion following deliberation at a moment of ethical demand (cf. Zigon 2007: 138). The young man in this case was of course way ahead of those who are absorbed by ambiguities and struggle with new situations and really concerned about their virtue. It should be noted that there were also participants in the association who totally disagreed with his argumentation and considered his behavior as moral neglect. The discussion at the mosque was also about breaking rules and virtue, but with a different stake. The central question was about how to interpret Islamic principles and authoritative codes of conduct in changing circumstances. Both in the case of the salat and in the case of the discussion about iftar in the mosque there is no consensus among practitioners about the implication of these normative rules and ethical boundaries. What is right or wrong becomes a topic for debate and controversy. This is the heart of the matter at stake.

Ethics reside firmly in the realm of everyday experiences. In that respect the emerging scholarly focus on "everyday religion" constitutes an important epistemological and methodological shift from institution to practice (Bowen 1998; Dessing et al. 2013). "Everyday religion" addresses the "bottom-up" experiences and religious practices of people of faith (Ammerman 2007; McGuire 2008). The concept of "everyday religion" builds on the postulate that theologies are not made exclusively in an official venue by religious experts, but at a multiplicity of places and occasions and not only by experts (Rappaport 1999; Orsi 2005). Expert religion is a specific domain of activity and reasoning, to be distinguished from the no less important religious activity of nonexperts— people who do not practice religion professionally (Davie 2006: 274).

Talal Asad (2012 [1986]) has referred to Islam as a discursive tradition in order to address this middle field. Tradition, he argues, has an authoritative status and it operates as an ethical guideline not because it has timeless qualities, but because it has come about as a result of a historical process of authentication of religious authority. In his words: "An Islamic discursive tradition is simply a tradition of Muslim discourse that addresses itself to conceptions of the Islamic past and future, with reference to a particular Islamic practice in the present. Clearly, not everything Muslims say and do belongs to an Islamic discursive tradition. Nor is an Islamic tradition in this sense necessarily imitative of what was done in the past" (ibid.). By firmly locating Islamic tradition into the realm of the everyday, Asad demonstrates that religious authority is a dynamic process of both critical reflection and constitution. If a discursive tradition is created by the generations of Muslims debating the correct form of practice with a view to its past, present and future, then acting Islamic is engaging with and acting upon this discursive tradition.

"Everyday religion" is thus an important methodological and epistemological step forward to understand the transition from the unity and authenticity of the word of God to the multiplicity and disputed quality of the words of mankind, to paraphrase Messick (1989: 28). However, this prompts us to answer the question of how to determine where moral acting begins and how it can be distinguished from "ordinary" acting, or whether this distinction makes sense altogether. Both the take on morality as a domain of dilemmas and choices, and an approach that focuses on ethical self-improvement provide no solution to this methodological problem. But also an approach that very explicitly includes failure as a constitutive element, as the editors of this volume propose to do, does not solve this problem. Failure and virtue are utterly ambiguous semantic categories subject to debate and contestation.

Morality is in most cases about bodily dispositions enacted in the world nonintentionally and unreflectively and comes close to Bourdieu's concept of habitus (Zigon 2007: 135). People normally do not think about their action in terms of morality, but their acting evolves according to normative scripts. Therefore to refer to the everyday situations in which Muslims find themselves as the domain of ethical ambiguity runs the risk of overemphasizing

Islam in what Muslims do and think (Schielke and Debevec 2012). Schielke and Debevec (2012) draw on De Certeau's (1984) notion of the everyday as the domain where ordinary Muslims confront the order and discipline of powerful institutions. "Everyday Islam" brings back the agency of ordinary Muslims (Mahmood 2005; Bracke 2008), and "tactical religion" as the domain of creativity and innovation, in constant interaction with dominant "strategic religion," which is "constantly engaged in operations to delimit and guard its sacred spaces" (Dessing et al. 2013: 35). This is a fruitful analytical alley, but it also turns morality into a field of contention and confrontation.

On the other hand, when looking at the recent literature that deals with "everyday Islam," or "lived Islam" it seems to me often too broad and hardly focused on ethical and normative issues. The ethical dissolves into the (Durkheimian) social and becomes no more than a cultural prerequisite. Lived Islam then tends to become shorthand for things people do whom we generically call Muslims. Is the individual performing his or her religious duties as much lived Islam as a football team consisting of people with an Islamic background? And can we call an organization founded by Muslims Islamic? There is thus a tendency to categorize activities and views of people with an Islamic background as Islamic without any thorough conceptual underpinning.

In other words, the question arises where lived Islam begins and where it ends. Is it possible to delineate this field of human activity? This prompts us to consider the distinction between "Islamic" and "non-Islamic." Lived Islam is not about the lives of Muslims as such, although an exploration of these lives constitutes a necessary aspect of lived Islam. Certain activities are Islamic not because they are performed by "Muslims," but because they are considered virtuous by certain Muslims. In that respect a football match may be conceived of as lived Islam and virtuous acting when the players and the organizers perceive it as such, provided they ethically underpin and authenticate their practices as religiously virtuous. On the other hand certain practices that are commonsensically categorized as religious, such as the salat or fasting, may not be performed with a deliberate religious motivation. The young man I referred to above argued that the set of ritual movements Muslims perform can only be called salat when they are performed out of sincerity and with the proper intention. In other words it should be a deliberate act otherwise the gestures remain empty and meaningless. The agency of Muslims must thus be a crucial prerequisite of analysis, just as the social embeddedness of the act.

Morality thus lies in practice, but individuals—however pious and devout they may be—will not continuously make a distinction between ethical acting and "ordinary" acting. At what moments and in what kinds of situations do ordinary routinely acting and making choices in familiar situations transform into moral acting? Where does nondeliberative acting transform into deliberative acting? This occurs in situations of high intensity and in situations of moral breakdown (Zigon 2007: 137). It occurs when ordinary situations and routine choices are problematized. Zigon calls this "an ethical moment" (2007: 137). Ordinary ethics become explicit in situations where breaches are experienced, where decisions are contested, or where an elite is making attempts to rationalize and canonize ethics (Lambek 2010: 2).

I take up this line of argumentation and further elaborate on it by making two crucial comments. First, when we consider failure constitutive of ethical self-improvement it is crucial to analyze the narrative, the explanation of the practitioner that comes with it. If a person explains his or her actions and ideas as erroneous, and consequently has feelings of failure, the personal explanation will indeed be in terms of straying from a path that is considered right and virtuous. The actor apparently has implicitly accepted the authoritative qualities of this path and abides to the rules about right and wrong that this path implicates. But in the case of my informant in the mosque who chose not to attend the salat, there was something else going on. He did explain his choice as a comment on the deeper layers of meaning behind religious duties and obligations and would probably not cast his motivations in a language of moral failure. My informant took issue with a, in his eyes, rather unreflective interpretation of Islamic principles.

Laidlaw offers an interesting perspective in this respect. According to him, agency in social science is understood either as a creative human force with transformative capacities, or as agency in the strict sense of the word, a causal force that brings about change (2010: 145). The latter approach is the guiding principle of "actor-network" approaches to be found in the work of Bruno Latour (see for example Latour 2005: 221). Agency need not necessarily be human. Laidlaw further elaborates on this second approach to agency, but argues that causality is not a neutral concept as if we deal with chemical reactions. What is causally significant, he argues, is a matter of explanation and interpretation. Here he brings in the concept of responsibility and argues: "Just as the adequacy of explanations of causality depends on the interests that motivate an inquiry, so attributions of responsibility depend upon interests, and what Strawson called the 'reactive attitudes' that characterize human interaction: reactive attitudes such as gratitude and resentment, indignation, approbation, guilt, shame, pride, hurt feelings, forgiveness, or love" (2010: 147). Responsibility, as we know, is a highly relevant concept in Islamic ethics (Hourani 1985; Brown 1999; Kloos, this volume; see also Ramadan 2008).[6] The extent to which certain acts are halal or haram is subject to complex theological deliberation and interpretation. Responsibility and agency are inherent aspects of this reasoning. So we might add to the range of reactive attitudes "being considered a virtuous agent."

Secondly, and following from the first comment, even if failure in whatever mode is constitutive of ethical formation, it still leaves the normative and authoritative frames that serve as a point of reference for virtuous acting untouched and undisputed, and thus reaffirms their authoritative status. Indeed Muslims in most cases abide to established Islamic rules and principles and attempt to live up to them. Their religious practices are therefore predominantly affirmative and reproductive.

However, experiences of failure in ethical self-improvement constitute an important aspect of religious subjectivation also because they may lead to reflexivity and eventually to a dispute about the deeper meanings of Islamic principles. When Muslims find themselves in changing social conditions, or when their daily lives are played out in different social settings—or in new and unprecedented situations that are difficult to reconcile with established traditions—frictions and ambiguities occur, and ordinary routines turn into dilemmas. These frictions may be experienced as failures to be able to live up to ethical requirements, but they might also lead to a critical reflection not just about one's individual ethical accomplishments, but also about the norms and principles themselves and the authoritative processes that undergird and reproduce them.

Creativity and Authentication: The Remaking of Religious Authority

Religious authority-making is a constant dynamic. It is not just an imposition of normative principles and regulations unto ordinary believers, but also a bottom-up critical reflection on their authoritative qualities. Historians of Islam and theologians can study how doctrinal developments in Islam have taken place, by analyzing theological sources, fatwas (legal opinions issued by a Muslim jurist), and other religious documents. With a rigorous historical and hermeneutical methodology they can lay bare how changes came about and how Islamic theology evolved. However, they tend to focus predominantly on material produced by religious experts, on canonized comments, authoritative documents, and scholarly debates. In other words, they study the very top end of the dynamic. There is hardly any insight into the religious activity of nonexperts and in the process that leads to doctrinal changes. There may be scholarly reflections on certain ethical issues, but there is virtually no evidence about the role of what I have called ordinary Muslims—that is, Muslims who find themselves in a dilemma that emerges from daily experiences and situations. Consequently, their input is predominantly ignored or deemed irrelevant.

This is of course understandable when it concerns historical research. We simply do not have any records of the societal processes and initiatives that preceded changes in Islamic law. I contend that any authoritative judgment is the result of reflections of ordinary Muslims and societal debates about pressing issues. Many of the analyses of doctrinal developments suffer from a reverse reading of doctrinal history and the tendency to turn consequences of certain developments into causes. By definition we have knowledge only of the outcomes of scholarly debates in the past and at best about rival interpretations, but we hardly have any insight into the processes that have led to certain theological decisions. An example may elucidate this. There is an abundance of material on fatwas and their implications (see e.g., Caeiro 2010). An analysis of fatwas gives us insight in how Islamic scholars decide on sensitive issues and how religious authorization of practices comes about. These fatwas are the doctrinal sediment, the consequences of societal developments. They come at the end of a process of debate, negotiation, and practice and indeed of innovation in which nonexperts, ordinary Muslims, play a crucial role. However, fatwas tend to be treated as causes of these developments, as the very beginning of religious change. This is too limited an approach.

Different experiences always lead to different interpretations of the same normative principles, but it may in some cases also lead to doctrinal change caused by dissolving legitimacy. When people find themselves in situations in which authoritative scripts are no longer self-evident or when a moral break-down occurs, transformation is likely to follow suit. Morality is always about stepping into an uncanny situation-at-hand and back once again into the unre-flective comfort of the familiar. "But this return from the ethical moment is *never a return to the same unreflective moral dispositions. …* It is in the moment of breakdown, then, that it can be said that people work on themselves, and in so doing, alter their very way of being-in-the-world" (Zigon 2007: 138, italics added). Two Muslims, one living all his or her life in a tiny remote village, the other in a big city in Europe, may refer to the same normative principles, but they have built up completely different ethical reference schemes. If one shares these experiences with others, a process that has been altered tremendously due to the use of modern media, we come closer to a reflection on the very authoritative status quo. Critical reflection may generate inventiveness and renewal and will impact on religious authentication, the social process that confers normative authority on persons, rules, or institutions.[7]

There are many indications that such a critical reflection is taking place among a growing number of Muslims in Europe and elsewhere for that matter, and has taken place perhaps for a longer period than is often assumed. It is commonly accepted that modernization, globalization and the emergence of modern mass media have unsettled traditional religious authority (Van Bruinessen 2003; Salvatore 2006, 2007; Mandaville 2007; Masud, Salvatore, and Van Bruinessen 2009; Caeiro 2010). Modern mass media have allowed for a tremendous increase in the number of voices in the public sphere (Eickelman and Anderson 2003: x; De Koning 2008). This has also affected Islamic author-ity in European countries. The authoritative frames and institutional settings that emerged in the early years of migration are still functioning, but their legitimacy is questioned by a growing number of Muslims born and raised in Europe (Peter 2006; Sunier 2014; Volpi and Turner 2007; cf. Watling 2002). A wide variety of issues of faith that were undisputed are now put into ques-tion. However, to attribute these developments simply to overarching societal transformations and modern communication technology ignores the ethical dimensions that are at play. But instead of remaining at a rather general and often abstract level of analysis, we should pay more attention to the very personal and individual level where reflections begin with ambiguities and dilemmas. The examples taken from my fieldwork I discussed all start with personal deliberation.

Today the sources of Islamic authority are more diverse and unstable than ever before. The authoritative and institutional frames of Islam in European countries, which have been developed under migratory conditions, are under pressure (Eickelman and Anderson 2003; Volpi and Turner 2007). Initiatives to set up institutes of religious learning or to develop organizational structures beyond ethnic dividing lines point in this direction. Also the rapidly increasing numbers of "new" independent preachers who are particularly popular among young Muslims are an indication of change. And there are all kinds of local initiatives to see how certain elements of Islamic law could be applied in society. There is a tendency to refer here only to radical voices in the public sphere because they challenge established religious authority most explicitly and vehemently. Many seem to forget that the vast majority of Muslims reflect on issues of faith and proper conduct and not just a radical minority.

There are a number of relevant domains where reflections, discussions and frictions are becoming more visible than before. Food in relation to religious norms and regulations is an ever widening field of debate and (commercial and religious) activity. The initiative by Muslims to develop a so-called halal quality mark in the Netherlands is an intriguing case in that respect. But halal certification implies not only food prescriptions and ritual slaughter; it is about expanding global markets for an increasingly wealthy pious middle class, including fashion and self-styling, consumer goods, art and entertainment (Moors 2009; Barendregt 2011; Fischer 2011). These expanding commercial activities generate new forms of religiosity and religious subjectivity; at least they constitute a new arena of ethical reflection. Religious authorities have to engage with these new forms and styles of religiosity.

Religious authority refers to the fundamental question as to who is entitled to speak legitimately on behalf of Islam and has persuasive qualities. This covers a wide range of issues. Already for quite some time a public debate has been going on about the qualities and legitimacy of imams in Europe and their position within the various Muslim communities. However, the legitimacy of these imams continues to be a sensitive issue. Cyber imams and wandering preachers are very popular because they wrap up their messages in a style and a rhetoric that appeals especially to young Muslims (De Koning 2008; Gräf and Skovgaard-Petersen 2009; Sunier 2011; Hirschkind 2012; Beekers 2015). This issue ties in with the more general development of building alternative religious communities across and beyond traditional ethnic, regional and doctrinal dividing lines. A very important issue is the position of women in matters of religious authority (cf. Jouili and Amir-Moazami 2006; Bano and Kalmbach 2011; Kloos and Künkler 2016).

A more general but nevertheless crucial issue concerns practices and initiatives that are related to personal relations in various forms. Some of the more sensitive issues that regularly appear in the press and are hotly discussed are partner choice, arranged marriages, forced marriages, divorce, interaction between young people of different sex, homosexuality, apostasy, and circumcision. All these issues constitute sensitive arenas of contestation and debate with strong ethical underpinnings. An adjacent field concerns processes of institutionalization of authority in matters of the application of *shari'a* (Islamic law). This is an even more sensitive issue because shari'a in the public image has become shorthand for violence and repression. However, there is a wide variety of initiatives and situations were "Islamic" rules are being applied to daily life, especially in family matters.

The question arises how dilemmas and reflections come about, how they turn into debates and initiatives, and how individual and collective agency is conducive in a process of authentication of religious authority. To address ethics properly, I argue, we have to trace the process in its entirety (full circle) and consider authentication as an intermediary step from individual reflection on ethical dilemmas and ambiguities to new religious authority and back. Various anthropologists have addressed the dynamics between everyday practices of ordinary Muslims on the one hand and "universal" Islamic normativity on the other. In order to capture this dynamic we need what Lambek calls a "political economy of knowledge" (1990). We need to study the local hermeneutics of religious sources and how they come about. Through ethnographic methods we need to unravel the complex and often fragmented process that leads to doctrinal change in which ordinary Muslims play a crucial but often neglected role.

Conclusion

There is hardly any insight into the question of how the religious activity of nonexperts affects processes of doctrinal change. This is the main observation I have elaborated in this chapter. Drawing on several fieldwork examples, I have argued that the very process of ethical deliberation around failure is not only constitutive of moral self-improvement, but may also lead to discussions about the deeper meaning of Islamic principles.

Let me, by way of a concluding remark, come back to my initial case of the discussion in the mosque in the city of Rotterdam. The relevance of the case for the issue at hand is twofold. First it shows that moral reflection and ethical ambiguity is not something new, but it has become more pressing in recent years. Secondly and more importantly it shows how the ways in which Islam takes shape in Europe is much more than a matter of institutional arrangements and agreements; it is a profoundly ethical issue. At the heart lies the dilemma about how to act in morally appropriate ways. The discussion in the mosque in Rotterdam back in the early 1990s is relevant because it points at the level of local everyday situations as the very beginning of ethical deliberation and eventually possible renewal. These discussions and deliberations are not at all trivial as some would argue, and they should be analyzed more thoroughly.

What is the relevance for the central theme of this volume? In their introduction, Kloos and Beekers state: "Our premise is that senses of failure offer an important and productive entry point for the study of lived religion in today's world, where religious commitments are often volatile, believers are regularly confronted by alternative lifestyles, worldviews or desires, and religious subjects tend to be self-reflexive." I have argued that I go along with this critical comment on analyses that exclusively focus on virtuous accomplishments and ignore the formative qualities of failure. I have drawn here on various anthropologists who have explored the middle way between everyday practices of Muslims and authoritative texts and frames and the dynamics between them. By doing so I have tried to elaborate on the ways in which individual experiences transform into altered collective ethics. The case of the iftar discussion in Rotterdam may in some way be understood as an elite discussion in which ordinary Muslims are only marginally involved. However, the case is indicative of an intriguing process of authentication of religious authority. Changing social circumstances prompt local collective actors in mosques to take steps, but while doing so they end up in a discussion that goes beyond practical considerations and touches on some crucial Islamic principles. By making decisions they do not only act as managers but also reconsider Islamic authority.

Thijl Sunier is an anthropologist and holds the chair of "Islam in European Societies" at VU University Amsterdam. He has conducted research on interethnic relations, Turkish youth and Turkish Islamic organizations in the Netherlands, comparative research among Turkish youth in France, Germany, Great Britain, and the Netherlands, and international comparative research on nation-building and multiculturalism in France and The Netherlands. Currently he works in the field of transnational Islamic movements and religious authority. He is chairman of the Dutch research school for Islamic Studies (NISIS). His latest book (with Nico Landman) is *Transnational Turkish Islam* (Palgrave Macmillan, 2015).

Notes

1. In this chapter I draw on examples taken from my ethnographic fieldwork over the past few decades.
2. For an elaborate discussion about the "public iftar," see Sunier 2012.
3. Quote from fieldwork notes 1990, Rotterdam.
4. Quote from fieldwork notes.
5. I prefer the somewhat problematic term "ordinary Muslim" over the more commonly used lay Muslims for want of a better term to denote those Muslims who are not religious experts or necessarily knowledgeable in matters of Islamic theology but bring into the analysis ordinary acting—acting in everyday situations. I critically engage with the dominant assumption that theological reflection is first and foremost a matter of theologians.
6. And as Joel Robbins and Leanne Williams Green note in their contribution to this volume, responsibility plays a crucial role in Christian ethics as well (cf. Van de Kamp, this volume).
7. I borrowed this term from Dorothea Schulz, who presented her current research on Islamic authorization in Mali at a conference in Utrecht, 26 June, 2014.

References

Ammerman, Nancy T. 2007. *Everyday Religion: Observing Modern Religious Lives.* Oxford: Oxford University Press.

Asad, Talal. 2012 [1986]. "The Idea of an Anthropology of Islam." In *The Anthropology of Islam Reader*, ed. Jens Kreinath, 93–111. London: Routledge.

Bano, Masooda, and Hilary Kalmbach. 2011. *Women, Leadership and Mosques: Changes in Contemporary Islamic Authority.* Leiden: Brill.

Barendregt, Bart. 2011. "Pop, Politics, and Piety: Nasyid Boy Band Music in Southeast Asia." In *Islam and Popular Culture in Indonesia and Malaysia*, ed. Andrew Weintraub, 235–256. London: Routledge.

Beekers, Daan. "A Moment of Persuasion: Travelling Preachers and Islamic Pedagogy in the Netherlands." *Culture and Religion* 16(2): 193–214.

Bowen, John. 1998. "Law and Social Norms in the Comparative Study of Islam." *The American Anthropologist* 100(4): 1034–1035.

Bracke, Sarah. 2008. "Conjugating the Modern-Religious, Conceptualizing Female Religious Agency: Contours of a 'Post-secular' Conjuncture." *Theory, Culture and Society* 25(6): 51–68.

Brown, Daniel. 1999. "Islamic Ethics in Comparative Perspective." *The Muslim World* 89(2): 181–192.

Caeiro, Alexandre. 2010. "The Power of European Fatwas: The Minority *Fiqh* Project and the Making of an Islamic Counterpublic." *International Journal of Middle East Studies* 42: 435–449.

Davie, Grace. 2006. "Religion in Europe in the 21st Century: The Factors to Take into Account." *European Journal of Sociology* 47(2): 271–296.

De Certeau, Michel. 1984. *The Practice of Everyday Life.* Berkeley, CA: University of California Press.

De Koning, Martijn. 2008. *Zoeken naar een 'Zuivere' Islam: Geloofsbeleving en Identiteitsvorming van Jonge Marokkaanse-Nederlandse Moslims.* Amsterdam: Bert Bakker.

Dessing, Nathal M., Nadia Jeldtoft, Jørgen S. Nielsen, and Linda Woodhead, eds. 2013. *Everyday Lived Islam in Europe.* Farnham and Burlington, VT: Ashgate.

Eickelman, Dale F., and Jon W. Anderson. 2003. *New Media and the Muslim World: The Emerging Public Sphere.* Bloomington and Indianapolis: Indiana University Press.

Fischer, Johan. 2011. *The Halal Frontier: Muslim Consumers in a Globalized Market.* New York: Palgrave Macmillan.

Gräf, Bettina, and Jacob Skovgaard-Petersen, eds. 2009. *Global Mufti: The Phenomenon of Yūsuf al-Qaraḍāwī.* London: Hurst.

Hirschkind, Charles. 2001. "The Ethics of Listening: Cassette-Sermon Audition in Contemporary Egypt." *American Ethnologist* 28(3): 623–649.

———. 2012. "Experiments in Devotion Online: The Youtube Khutba." *International Journal of Middle East Studies* 44: 5–21.

Hourani, George F. 1985. *Reason and Tradition in Islamic Ethics.* Cambridge: Cambridge University Press.

Jouili, Jeanette, and Schirin Amir-Moazami. 2006. "Knowledge, Empowerment and Religious Authority among Pious Muslim Women in France and Germany." *Muslim World* 96: 617–642.

Kloos, David, and Mirjam Künkler. 2016. "Studying Female Islamic Authority: From Top-Down to Bottom-Up Modes of Certification." *Asian Studies Review* 40(4): 479–490.

Laidlaw, James. 2010. "Agency and Responsibility: Perhaps You Can Have Too Much of a Good Thing." In *Ordinary Ethics: Anthropology, Language and Action*, ed. Michael Lambek, 143–165. New York: Fordham University Press.

Lambek, Michael J. 1990 "Certain Knowledge, Contestable Authority: Power and Practice on the Islamic Periphery." *American Ethnologist* 17(1): 23–40.

Lambek, Michael J., ed. 2010. *Ordinary Ethics: Anthropology, Language and Action*. New York: Fordham University Press.

Latour, Bruno. 2005. *Reassembling the Social*. Cambridge: Cambridge University Press.

Mahmood, Saba. 2005. *Politics of Piety: The Islamic Revival and the Feminist Subject*. Princeton, NJ: Princeton University Press.

Mandaville, Peter. 2007. "Globalization and the Politics of Religious Knowledge." *Theory, Culture and Society* 24(2): 101–105.

Masud, Muhammad K., Armando Salvatore, and Martin van Bruinessen, eds. 2009. *Islam and Modernity: Key Issues and Debates*. Edinburgh: Edinburgh Press.

McGuire, Meredith B. 2008. *Lived Religion: Faith and Practice in Everyday Life*. Oxford: Oxford University Press.

Messick, Brinkley. 1989. "Just Writing: Paradox and Political Economy in Yemeni Legal Documents." *Cultural Anthropology* 4(1): 26–50.

Moors, Annelies. 2009. "'Islamic Fashion' in Europe: Religious Conviction, Aesthetic Style, and Creative Consumption." *Encounters* 1(1): 175–201.

Orsi, Robert A. 2005. *Between Heaven and Earth: The Religious Worlds People Make and the Scholars Who Study Them*. Princeton: Princeton University Press.

Peter, Frank. 2006. "Individualization and Religious Authority in Western European Islam." *Islam and Christian-Muslim Relations* 17(1): 105–118.

Ramadan, Tariq. 2008. *Radicale hervorming: islamitische ethiek en bevrijding*. Amsterdam: Van Gennep.

Rappaport, Roy. 1999. *Ritual and Religion in the Making of Humanity*. Cambridge: Cambridge University Press.

Salvatore, Armando. 2006. "Power and Authority within European Secularity: From Enlightenment Critique of Religion to the Contemporary Presence of Islam." *Muslim World* 96: 543–561.

———. 2007. "Authority in Question: Secularity, Republicanism and 'Communitarianism' in the Emerging Euro-Islamic Public Sphere." *Theory, Culture and Society* 24(2): 135–160.

Schielke, Samuli, and Debevec, Liza, eds. 2012. *Ordinary Lives and Grand Schemes: An Anthropology of Everyday Religion*. New York and Oxford: Berghahn Books.

Sunier, Thijl. 1996. *Islam in beweging: Turkse jongeren en islamitische organisaties*. Amsterdam: Het Spinhuis.

———. 2011. "New Religious Leadership among Muslims in Europe." *Australian Religion Studies Review* 24(3): 275–296.

———. 2012. "Nationale Iftar: de vermaatschappelijking van een ritueel." in *Feesten in Multi-Etnisch Nederland*, ed. Irene Stengs, 57–77. Amsterdam: Amsterdam University Press.

———. 2014. "Domesticating Islam: Exploring Knowledge Production on Islam in European Societies." *Ethnic and Racial Studies* 37(6): 1138–1155.

Van Bruinessen, Martin. 2003. "Making and Unmaking Muslim Religious Authority in Western Europe." The Fourth Mediterranean Social and Political Research Meeting, Robert Schuman Centre for Advanced Studies, European University Institute, Florence, 19–23 March.

Volpi, Frédéric, and Bryan S. Turner. 2007. "Making Islamic Authority Matter." *Theory, Culture and Society* 24(2): 1–19.

Watling, Tony. 2002. "Leadership or Dialogue? Authority and Religious Change in a Netherlands Community." *Sociology of Religion* 63(4): 515–539.

Zigon, Jarrett. 2007. *Morality: An Anthropological Perspective*. Oxford: Berg.

EPILOGUE
Religion, Lived Religion, and the "Authenticity" of Failure

Mattijs van de Port

Whenever students come to me with research plans to study one or the other dimension of "religion," I suggest they make a barbershop the prime locale of their fieldwork. They often think I am joking, but that is not the case. What I hope they take from my suggestion is to rethink their impulse to situate a research on religion in a temple, church, shrine, or mosque. Clearly, in such places one may engage in conversations with the truly devoted, be they priests, or recent converts, or other types of enthusiasts. And obviously, there is a lot to be learned from such engaged interlocutors. Yet in anthropological work on religion the practices and viewpoints of the pious, the truly devoted and the zealots too often come to stand for the religion at large.

In a barbershop, I tell my students you can witness how religious practices are entangled with other concerns of the everyday (having a cool haircut, for instance); how a person's religious identification plays itself out vis-a-vis other identifications (with the popstars or actors or football players whose portraits may hang on the wall); how religion enters and disappears from ongoing conversations. In other words, religion as lived is not the same as religion as talked about. And, as David Kloos and Daan Beekers show in their introduction to this volume, ever more anthropologists maintain that when you study the way religion is lived, you have to take notice of the plurality of moral frameworks that are at play in people's lives.

Studying lived religion also draws attention to the fluctuating intensities of religious identifications. For "being a Muslim," "being a Christian" (or in my own research on Bahian Candomblé: "being a devotee of the Orixá spirits") not only means different things for different people; it also means different things for the same person in different situations. To encounter religion in the everyday is to note the never-ending modulations of religious declarations: jubilant at the height of Holy Mass; indifferent when plagued by a hangover; doubtful in the waiting room of a clinic; or simply absent when involved in those simple, everyday activities that call for full concentration. Studying lived religion involves questions such as: how Catholic is the Catholic seamstress at the moment of sewing a complicated dress? How Islamic is the cook as he cuts his vegetables? How Buddhist is the monk trying to figure out new software on his computer? Were you to ask them, they would probably say: "of course I am Catholic, or Muslim, or Buddhist." Yet the point is that this answer—and concomitant identification—appears because of the question being asked. In the here and now of sewing, cooking, and studying software, religiosity may have been numbed to the point of being indiscernible.

Many religions put themselves out there as all-encompassing life programs, and introduce disciplinary practices that work toward the complete "take over" of body and soul. Think of the iconic scene of a baptism taking place in a river, where a convert is pushed under water, so as to ensure that the baptism takes in all of her, from head to toe. That scene captures the totalizing aspirations of religions. A study of lived religion, however, shows the limits of such pretensions. It highlights that the making of religious subjects is always a work in progress. Religious identities are always in scaffolds. Religiously claimed bodies are always more than what a religion wants out of them. Indeed, the one example that I can think of that might be taken as a lifelong prolongation of the baptism in the river would be monastic life—yet the very institution of the monastery, with its walls and seclusion, only underscores just how hard a full realization of totalizing religious life programs is.

It is only recently that anthropologists of religion have begun to pay attention to the fluctuating intensities of religious identifications. The conventions of research design, which require that informants are a priori labeled as pertaining to a particular religious category ("I'm going to study Muslims," "I'm going to study Christians"), are not particularly helpful to bring out this dimension of lived religion. When we address our interlocutors in their capacity as religious subjects, we tend to reinforce the totalizing frames religions seek to impose. If an informant is buying shoes, we observe a religious person buying shoes. If he is running a marathon, we observe a religious person running a marathon. When we ask them about modern art, we search out their stories for matter that is religiously relevant. The religious label becomes the cohering force of our studies; it is what keeps our narratives together. But do we thus catch the instability of religious identities, the fluctuating intensities of being "religious"?

I have to admit, I usually fail to convince my students to do an ethnography of barbershop religion. To my knowledge, it still needs to be written. So

I was all the more pleased with the invitation to read the contributions to this volume. In their introduction, Kloos and Beekers reject the interpretation of religion as a "pervasive, uniform or constant force" in the lives of believers and suggest scholars of religion ought to scrutinize what goes on when religious aspirations meet up with the contingencies of everyday life. The different chapters offer a rich sample of ethnographically informed case studies.

It is interesting to note that the editors' intention to focus on lived religion first and foremost yields the idea to concentrate on the effects of self-perceived "moral failure." The everyday is brought into view as a domain of disruption, threatening to throw religious propositions about how to live a good life, and be a good person, in disarray. I agree that the sense of "having failed" is part and parcel of religion as it is lived (and indeed, such failures are recognized and addressed in religious discourses and practices). Yet I kept thinking we should also keep in mind that the everyday produces moments when religious propositions about life and being appear to be in sync with the actual experiences of the faithful—blissful moments in which the world fully complies with religious narrations of it, and "seem tailor-made for one another," as Terry Eagleton (2009: 10) would put it. These moments may be fleeting, but they offer the satisfaction of religious propositions "fully making sense," and may become important anchor points on which to ground religious identifications. Clear examples are found in Daan Beekers' chapter, where interlocutors recall the good times when they started the day with prayer, or the peace of mind they experienced during pilgrimage.

Having said that, all the chapters in the volume show in one way or another that everyday experiences of moral failure play an important role in the formation of religious subjects. Joel Robbins and Leanne Williams Green liken failure to the "engine" of religious life, a metaphor that aptly captures the idea that a sense of failure may move religious subjects into action. In their chapter, they show how failure intensifies the monitoring of "inner" moral shortcomings or keeps up the readiness to fight off demonic attacks. From Martijn de Koning's contribution on Salafi Muslims in the Netherlands we learn that a sense of failure fuels the drive to realize a further perfection of one's personal piety, a point that also comes to the fore in Daan Beekers' chapter on young Muslims and Christians in the Netherlands. Linda van de Kamp's Mozambican findings show how the sense of failure stimulates believers to reframe their own role in the pursuit of prosperity in Maputo, while Thijl Sunier, discussing Muslims in Western Europe, shows how experiences of failure trigger "reflection, inventiveness, and renewal" with regard to the requirements of Islamic normative frames. David Kloos' contribution, which discusses religious negligence and the responses it generates in Aceh, Indonesia, forms an interesting counterpoint to the other chapters. It highlights a popular understanding that religious commitments do indeed fluctuate from person to person, and from life stage to life stage. His interlocutors do not make too much of a fuss over such fluctuations, confident that with the coming of age, people's commitment to their religion will intensify.

Now where might the insights brought up in this volume take us in the anthropological study of lived religion? Where do we move from here? What research trajectories are opened up? Kloos and Beekers use the findings brought together in this volume to break an ever more paralyzing deadlock in the study of religious practices, moralities, and subjectivities. They argue that the study of the pursuit of ethical perfection (as found in the works of Talal Asad, Saba Mahmood, and others) is too often (and unproductively) pitted against the study of the ambivalences of everyday religion (as discussed in the work of Samuli Schielke and others). In reality, however, moral failures are part and parcel of processes of ethical formation. In what follows, I would like to expand on these thoughts by discussing how failure is an inescapable given in human world-making tout court.

Let me start with an observation. I noticed that, while reading the contributions, I experienced a certain sense of relief. Going through the notes that I scribbled in the margins of the manuscript, I find myself writing (too hastily perhaps): "nothing more human than failure" and "the focus on failure is a deeply humanizing move." Those scribblings already indicate what this sense of relief refers to.

With the rise of religious (and other) fundamentalisms and orthodoxies in the contemporary world, totalizing discourses on life and being are everywhere. It seems to me that the appeal of these discourses—and their presence in the public sphere—must be understood as a symptom of the loss of certainty in our media-saturated societies and wired-up worlds. Truths that used to provide guidelines for living have become "opinions." One's take on reality is always already disputed by someone else's, and can no longer be taken for granted. Totalizing discourses promise a renewed sense of certainty. Media logics, which privilege clear, outspoken opinions over expressions of ambiguity, or even doubt, give the impression that increasing numbers of people have managed to convince themselves to be in possession of religious certainties. That, in my perception of things, produces a frightening spectacle. Hence my sense of relief: anthropological accounts that counter such media-produced impressions speak to my liberal worldview. I have great difficulties in imagining the desire to make oneself over to the teachings of one Holy Scripture or another: pertaining to what Charles Taylor called "a culture of authenticity" (Taylor 1989). I was brought up to believe that figuring out one's own destiny in the light of one's personal characteristics and talents is the adventure that makes life worth living. Failure is an inextricable part of that adventure. You try, you fail, you learn, you try again, or you try something else.

Allow me to share with you an example, which vividly illustrates the warm feelings confrontations with failure produce in me. When recently song writer Bob Dylan was awarded the Nobel Prize for literature, singer Patty Smith was contracted to go to Oslo to pick up the prize on his behalf, and she performed one of his songs. There she stood, amidst gala dressed royalty, ambassadors, and dignitaries. Smith too wore a black and white suit, but her long grey hair, uncombed, hippy-like, served as a strong reminder of her wilder, rebellious soul. Her rendition of Dylan's "A Hard Rain's A-Gonna Fall" was impressive: a raw, emotional voice piercing the groomed and polished world where it was made to resound. But then she failed. She lost her lines. She had to stop the music, and apologize. Blushing, she said she was so nervous. She then moved on. Gloriously, all the way to the last strophe. This failure really touched me, as it broke up the decorum, undid the stiff formality of the occasion, and allowed a "more human" note to come into being. Judging by the long and warm applause the singer received, many people in the audience were as moved as I by this performance.

What this example teaches about the sense of relief I felt when reading the contributions to this volume is that it follows a very particular, secular perspective on life that equates failure with "authenticity," and which dismisses a submission to pregiven religious scripts for living as "make-belief" and therefore "inauthentic." I am enough of an anthropologist to know that my own feelings are probably irrelevant to the people that figure in the chapters of this book. And yet, I am not quite willing to just drop this theme of the "authenticity of failure." First of all because I think I had better be transparent about the way my scholarly voice has been shaped inside and out of academia, and my understandings of totalizing discourses on life and being are not unbiased. Second, because the "authenticity of failure" speaks to perspectives on human world-making that I will discuss below and which take the incompleteness of all forms of sense-making as a starting point for analysis. And third, because an encounter with religious subjects who are not selling the anthropologist the dreamed-up version of their creed, but show us to be trying, failing, learning, and trying again might provide a much-needed common ground between anthropologist and interlocutor, and more broadly, between adherents of religious and secular world readings.

Following this train of thought I will suggest two paths for further research, both of which, as mentioned, try to bring out dynamics of world-making that transcend religious or secular particulars. One trajectory would invoke a Lacanian-informed scholarship that broadens the notion of failure as an existential given in all human world-making. The other would bring in recent scholarship on affect, which teaches us that human bodies are unruly presences in people's lives, prone to add to senses of failure.

The Lacanian framework of analysis starts from the premise that inherent in any narration of life and being is an unavoidable lack. Some scholars, like Cornelius Castoriadis, understand this lack as the ultimate contingency of the social constitution of the world. He noted how society always attempts to cover over the traces of this contingency by "presenting itself as the product of a pre-social or extra-social, and thus eternal and unchanging or foundational source. Gods, heroes or ancestors are the likeliest candidates, and, more recently, the so-called laws of nature or laws of history" (cited in Stavrakakis 2007: 42). Other Lacanian thinkers highlight how lack is produced by the structuring principles underlying symbolic orders, which are incapable of capturing the plenum of existence, which in Lacanian terminology is called the Real. Thus, in *The Sublime Object of Ideology* (1989), Slavoj Žižek describes human world-making as "a process which mortifies, drains off, empties, carves the fullness of the Real" (1989: 169). But then he points out that this Real is at the same time "the product, remainder, leftover, scraps of this process of symbolization" (ibid.: 169): an unavoidable reality surplus that comes into being as we seek to impose symbolic orders on life and being. Unassimilable, this reality surplus unrelentingly besieges the fortresses of meaning, threatening the stability of cultural (and religious) definitions of what is possible, normal, credible, or true. In more experiential, subjective terms, the Real is that which is in excess to our imagined selves: the thoughts we cannot think, the feelings we cannot feel, the impulses upon which we cannot act if we are to remain who we think we are. Terry Eagleton likens it with "a kind of foreign body lodged inside us"; an "alien wedge" at the core of our being that prohibits us from being at one with our identities.

Lacanian thinkers invite scholars of religion to study human subjects as reaching to fully find themselves in religious identities, but underscore that such reaching is bound to fail, given that the subject is always more than what a religion wants to make out of him or her. Starting out from the inevitable, in-built "failure" of identity formations, they have generated a whole range of questions related to how human beings handle this lack, which might reinvigorate the study of religiously motivated action. What is the role of utopian fantasies in screening off the lack in religious narratives and religious practices? What needs to be repressed in the subject to become a true follower of the Faith, and in what guises does the repressed return? What happens when utopian fantasies wear off, and what is the role of desire in creating ever new utopias? The dynamics that such questions seek to unearth are not really limited to religious discourses, but shape all attempts to carve meaningful worlds out of the plenum of existence.

Which brings me to a second direction, where I would take the findings of this volume: the unruly body as a continuous source of failure. Bodies involved in religious practices often strike me as routine. Bodies that pray, perform ritual washings, kiss holy icons, sing psalms, sit still in contemplation come across as bodies in coordinated, purposeful action, bodies that know what they want from these movements, and act to get it. Affect theory, however, teaches us that bodies are always in excess of what we want from them—religiously or otherwise. There is always an experiential surplus to the activities they engage in. Indeed, to talk about "the body" in unified terms—as we often do with great facility—is misleading, and in denial of what goes on inside our bodies at any single moment of the day: multiple sensations and experiences, all happening at the same time. It is in that sense that bodies fail us. No matter how bodies are interpellated—by discourses, rituals, sensational forms—they are always in excess of the forms such interpellations offer. The infinite number of processes going on inside the body, and between the body and the world, are never wholly captured. This experiential surplus of the interpellated body may be muted, but it is therefore not gone. To the contrary, it keeps prompting alternative awarenesses, experiences and feelings, which may produce dissonances in religious practices: disturb, distract, complicate, obstruct, or inspire the religious subject to act differently. Unwilling to comply with religious self-understandings, the experiential surplus bodies produce may cast doubt on the sincerity of a believer's actions, or raise an awareness of his hypocrisy.

Debates in phenomenological anthropology and cultural analysis have pondered this unruly body that can never be fully controlled by religious or other interpellations. Brian Massumi, for instance, in his studies on the notion of "affect," highlights the multiple experiential processes going on inside our bodies. His analysis invites us to keep this multiplicity in focus, observing how it constantly plays up as an ineradicable ambiguity in all our attempts to make sense of the world and of ourselves. "Affect," he says, is a "domain of intensity, indeterminacy, and above all potentiality, which the signifying logic of culture reduces" (cited in Mazzarella 2009: 293). Just how adequate the notion of affect is for the study of fluctuating intensities of religiosity comes to the fore in the following quote:

> In culture theory, people often talk as if the body on the one hand, and our emotions, thoughts, and the language we use for them on the other, are totally different realities, as if there has to be something to come between them and put them into touch with each other. This mediation is the way a lot of theorists try to overcome the old Cartesian duality between mind and body, but it actually leaves it in place and just tries to build a bridge between them. [What we need to come to terms with is that] there's an affect associated with every functioning of the body, from moving your foot to take a step to moving your lips to make words. Affect is … the body passing out of the present moment and the situation it's in, towards the next one. … You can think of affect in the broadest sense as what remains of the body's potential after each or everything a body says or does—as a perpetual bodily remainder. (Massumi 2015: 34)

Again, the theme of a surplus to world-making, now encountered at the level of bodily sensations and affect—the "perpetual bodily remainder"—sensitizes the scholar of religion to an inherent "perpetual" failure of totalizing discourses. Massumi's understanding of affect prohibits the idea that a constant honing of the body would in the end produce "a religious subject." The body he offers up for thought is and remains a treacherous body, an infinite potential for promiscuous engagements with alternative identifications, for religious failure. Massumi thus brings us back to the theme of religiosity as an ever wavering curve of intensities, peaking in moments, dropping at other moments, depending on the particular ways in which the body of a religious subject is being addressed as it moves in and out of religious settings. Questions one could ask with his theory in mind are: What are the conditions under which the body is being addressed? Does a particular setting allow for attentiveness and concentration? How is it that the multiple experiential processes that the notion of affect brings to our attention distract bodies that are religiously interpellated in one or the other religious setting?

By bringing in the "perpetual bodily remainder," affect theory helps us to ponder the role of the body in the experiences of failure discussed in this volume. In line with Kloos and Beekers' idea that the sense of failure is also a generative force in the making of religious subjects, Massumi considers this unruly bodily remainder to be as necessary a dimension of human sense-making as the body that does respond to religious interpellations. Affect, he writes, is "like a reserve of potential or newness or creativity that is experienced alongside every actual production of meaning in language or performance … — vaguely but directly experienced, as something more, a more to come, a life overspilling as it gathers itself up to move on." Following up on this thought, one might say that affect—here understood as life overspilling the forms in which it is cast—may be exactly what gives totalizing religious discourses their persuasive force: far from being a mere blueprint or mold to which one has to submit oneself, it is affect that turns them into an eternal becoming.

Both Lacanian-inspired cultural analysis and affect theory point to failure as a given with human existence. Highlighting dynamics of world-making that transcend the particularities of religious, nationalist, academic, humanist, anthropological or whatever other narrations of life and being, they show failure—and the need to act upon it—to be an "authentically" human affair. Research along these lines may provide that much-needed common ground between religious and secular world readings.

Mattijs van de Port works as an anthropologist at the University of Amsterdam and VU University Amsterdam. At the latter institution he holds the chair of "popular religiosity." He did research on the seductions of violence in the war-ridden Serbia of the 1990s, on which he published an ethnographic monograph, *Gypsies, Wars and other Instances of the Wild* (Amsterdam University Press, 1998). Since 2001, he does research in Bahia, Brazil, where he studies the afro-Brazilian religion Candomblé, which resulted in his study *Ecstatic Encounters: Bahian Candomblé and the Quest for the Really Real* (Amsterdam University Press, 2011) and a number of ethnographic films, including the essay-film *The Possibility of Spirits* (2016).

References

Eagleton, Terry. 2009. *Trouble with Strangers*. Chichester: Wiley & Blackwell.
Massumi, Brian. 2015. *Politics of Affect*. Cambridge: Polity Press.
Mazzarella, William. 2009. "Affect: What is it Good For?" In *Enchantments of Modernity: Empire, Nation, Globalization*, ed. Saurabh Dube, 291–310. New Delhi: Routledge.
Stavrakakis, Yannis. 2007. *The Lacanian Left: Essays on Psychoanalysis and Politics*. Albany: State University of New York Press.
Taylor, Charles. 1989. *Sources of the Self: The Making of Modern Identity*. Cambridge: Cambridge University Press.
Žižek, Slavoj. 1989. *The Sublime Object of Ideology*. London: Verso.

INDEX

sensation 129–130
sexuality, 33, 58, 92, 101
shame, 64, 101, 115
shari'a. *See* Islamic law
shortcoming, 2, 11, 13, 93, 95, 103, 126
shyness, 4, 45
sin, 2, 11–13, 22–26, 26–28, 30–31, 33, 46, 49–50, 76, 80, 97, 103, 110, 112. *See also* original sin
sincerity, 13, 37–38, 41–43, 45, 49–50, 56, 59, 97, 99, 103, 104n6, 110, 114, 129
sinfulness. *See* sin
sinner, 26
skepticism, 10–11
soul, 23, 125, 127
spirit, 22, 24, 26–34, 57–58, 61, 63, 95, 125. *See also* evil spirit; Holy Spirit
spirituality, 22, 28–31, 33, 48, 55, 58–59, 61, 63, 67, 76, 78, 86, 96–97
state, the, 11, 44, 67, 92, 95–96, 103, 104n4,
struggle, 2, 11, 13–14, 25–26, 33, 38, 43, 49, 63, 72–74, 76–80, 82, 93, 110, 112
Sub-Saharan Africa, 22, 24, 27–34. *See also* Africa
Sufism, 102
sunna, 45
supplication (Islamic). See *du'a*
synagogue, 10
Syria, 43, 46

The Netherlands, 10, 13, 14, 35n2, 37–39, 45, 68n7, 72–75, 78, 82–83, 85–86, 104n5, 112, 118, 126

technology, 30, 78, 81, 117
temporality, 77, 80, 86, 103
temptation, 13, 22, 27–28, 38, 43–44, 47–48, 51, 76, 111
traditional African religions, 57
transnationalism, 57
Trinity, 22
truth, 1–2, 10, 42–44, 46, 48–49, 127
Turkey, 78

ulama, 95
umma, 38, 43, 45–46, 48, 95, 101
unbelief, 42
uncertainty, 1, 8, 10–11, 38, 40–41, 47, 49, 67, 93–94, 99

violence, 46, 50, 91, 95, 101, 118
virtue, 2, 4, 12–13, 33, 42, 49, 110–115, 119

war, 23, 43, 45–47, 50, 67, 91
wealth, 27, 55, 58, 60 63, 65–67, 68n15, 99, 118. *See also* prosperity
Weber, Max, 68n6
Western world, the, 45, 81
witchcraft, 29, 57
wrongdoing, 32, 86

yoga, 85
Yoruba, the, 30–31, 33
young people, 23, 68n18, 81, 118
youth, 23, 40, 75, 93, 98–99

Zigon, Jarrett, 111–114, 117
Žižek, Slavoj, 128

www.ingramcontent.com/pod-product-compliance
Lightning Source LLC
Chambersburg PA
CBHW062109040426
42336CB00042B/2701